KINDER SCOUT

Portrait of a Mountain

This book is dedicated to the memory of Benny Rothman who led
the Mass Trespass of 1932 and died on 23rd January 2002

Kinder Scout - Portrait of a Mountain. 1st edition 2002
Published by Derbyshire County Council, Libraries and Heritage Department in partnership
with the National Trust and the Peak District National Park
Text Copyright 2002. Derbyshire County Council, Libraries and Heritage Department

ISBN 0 903463 68 7

Design Mike Dunmore. Repro Prestige Filmsetters
Printed by Raithby Lawrence at the De Montfort Press, Leicester
Sole Distributor. Cordee 3a DeMontfort Street, Leicester LE1 7HD. www.cordee.co.uk

EDITED BY ROLY SMITH

CONTENTS

A Kinder Child

FOREWORD BY SIR MARTIN DOUGHTY

STEPHEN'S STONES

PHOTO ESSAY BY STEPHEN LEWIS

THE WEEPING MAN BY STEPHEN LEWIS

SIR MARTIN DOUGHTY, CHAIRMAN OF ENGLISH NATURE & THE PEAK DISTRICT NATIONAL PARK AUTHORITY

I grew up and have now returned to live in New Mills, a small market town which enjoys what I believe are the best middle-distance views of Kinder Scout. Significant parts of the parish around Rowarth lie within the Peak District National Park, and it was here in 1932 that the late Benny Rothman and his colleagues planned their famous assault on Kinder, which was to act as such an important catalyst for the national parks and access to the countryside movement.

After their arrest – which was witnessed by my father when he was a 15-year-old youth – they were held in the cells at New Mills police station overnight. Benny returned to the town in much happier circumstances in 1994 to unveil a plaque to commemorate the trespass and his temporary incarceration in the town.

Kinder has always held a fascination for me. When I was a lad, it was a tradition in New Mills to walk over to Edale on Good Friday, and often to walk back again as well, if the Nag's Head had proved too hospitable!

Now a year after the 50th anniversary of the creation of the first UK national park here in the Peak District, we have new legislation to enshrine in law the freedom to roam on the moorland of Kinder Scout. The Peak was the only National Park to unequivocally back the need to legislate, based on our experience of the past 50 years trying to get access by agreement. Almost half of the eligible land is still closed off today, but the passing of the Countryside and Rights of Way Act will put that right.

THE WATCHER

I am delighted that the inspiration for this book came from another New Mills resident, Stephen Lewis, a town council gardener, who originally put together a wonderful exhibition of his photographs of Kinder Scout in the town's Heritage Centre.

Sir Martin Doughty

THE MOAT STONES

The idea for this book originated from an exhibition of photographs by Stephen Lewis which was staged at the New Mills Heritage Centre in 2001. Stephen, the assistant manager of the Parks and Leisure Department of New Mills Town Council, has known Kinder as a walker all his life, but his interest in photography is fairly recent. *"I sort of slipped into it,"* he explained, *"I bought a camera, then got a better one, and found that I enjoyed recording the different aspects of Kinder."*

BOXING GLOVE STONES

THE SNAIL

CHARLES COTTON DESCRIBING THE PEAK IN THE WONDERS OF THE PEAKE (1681)
A Country so Deform'd, the Traveller, would swear those parts Nature's Pudenda were:
Like Warts and Wens, Hills on the one side swell,
To all but Natives Inaccessible.

The Kinder Caper

INTRODUCTION BY ROLY SMITH

LOOKING DOWN FROM THE DOWNFALL TOWARDS KINDER RESERVOIR

I can never hear Ralph Vaughan Williams's *'Fantasia on a Theme by Thomas Tallis'* without thinking about Kinder Scout. It's an association of ideas, of course, because it instantly takes me back to the days in the mid-1970s when I was an information assistant doing weekend duties at the Fieldhead Visitor Centre of the Peak District National Park at Edale.

Our designer had just completed an audio-visual slide-tape programme which brilliantly expressed her personal love affair with the mountain, and that was the music she had chosen to go with it. To be fair, it fitted the programme and the mountain very well, perfectly expressing the sombre majesty of the highest point in the Peak.

The a.v. theatre adjoined the information desk, but we'd made the mistake of allowing visitors to start the programme for themselves on demand by pressing a button. The programme lasted for about 25 minutes, and of course, it was played constantly as people watched it, or by children who idly pressed the button, got bored, and walked out.

So when those quietly ecstatic, rhapsodic passages start ringing in my ears, I'm instantly transported to the tors and moors and the cloughs and groughs of Kinder Scout, and I suspect I always will be.

Like many walkers before me and I'm certain many more since, I'll never forget my first encounter with Kinder Scout. It was the early 70s, and I had escaped the choking confines of strike-torn Coventry with a fellow journalist for a day's walking in the Peak. I remember the paper's somewhat supercilious drama critic asking us, in all innocence, who was this more benevolent member of the popular boys' youth movement we were meeting in Derbyshire? Apart from knowing how to pronounce the name correctly, we didn't know much more about Kinder than him at the time. Neither of us had been there before, but I'd read up what looked like an interesting route delineated by Walter Poucher in that scratchy white pen which was my introduction to the hills in the days long before I could read a map.

We set off from the neat hamlet of Barber Booth and into the gradually narrowing ravine of Crowden Brook. There was, and still is, a feeling of a Highland glen in the grand interlocking spurs to this approach to Kinder, and it remains one of my favourites.

VARIOUSLY KNOWN AS THE MUSHROOM GARDEN OR WHIPSNADE, THE OLDER AND MORE CORRECT NAME IS THE WOOLPACKS

Graceful rowans wept over tumbling waterfalls as the route soon gave way to rough gritstone boulders and we walked up into the silent, beating heart of the hills, watched over all the time by the looming buttresses of Crowden Tower. Occasional light showers of rain did not deter us, for there was the promise of sun to come. An exciting little scramble near the infamous Keyhole Rock eventually brought us breathlessly out onto the summit plateau.

What a sight greeted our unbelieving eyes! We had never seen anything remotely like *this* before, and we were simply not prepared for it.

Simultaneously, we both reflected we could have been on the Moon. A vast, rippling sea of peat hags and groughs stretched to the far horizon, with not a sign of vegetation nor life of any kind. Paradoxically, we felt on top of the world but at the same time as if we were looking at an ocean of chocolate-coloured breakers of peat.

Then as the promised watery sun broke through the clouds, thin wisps of steam began to rise gently from the endless banks of peat. Kinder really was like John Hillaby had described it – *"a vast heap of dinosaur droppings."*

The only sound to break the oppressive,

primeval silence of this soggy wilderness was the now-familiar, 'go back, go back' warning cackle of a brace of red grouse, and the faint cheep of meadow pipits sounding, again as Hillaby had put it, *"like the last ticks of a clock that has almost run down."*

Of course, I've been back many, many times since, and old Kinder has never let me down. It's always the same, yet somehow always different. Unfailingly big, moody and magnificent, Kinder Scout is truly more of a spirit than a mountain.

*I*t exercises such an overpowering, all-pervading influence on its surroundings that it is still repeatedly, but incorrectly, named on some modern maps simply as 'The Peak.' As Paddy Monkhouse, one of its finest chroniclers, pointed out, the Peak is a district, not a mountain. In any case, he added, anything less like the dictionary definition of a peak would be hard to find.

This indefinable spiritual presence, shared with other hills like Coniston Old Man and Ben Nevis, imparts an air of mysticism to Kinder for many people. At least one organisation regards Kinder as a sacred mountain. George King, founder and president of the Aetherus Society,

chose Kinder as one of the world summits during his 'Operation Starlight' between 1958 and 1961. For his believers it is a potential storehouse for cosmic forces, and for those who know where to find it, there is a 'charged rock' inscribed with mysterious symbols among Cluther Rocks on the western side of the hill, overlooking the watery eye of Kinder Reservoir. This is apparently where the faithful will gather on the day of judgement to be transported to a different, but surely no more beautiful, world.

Just visible from Cluther Rocks is the fabled Mermaid's Pool, a dark and brooding tarn which promises immortality to anyone who encounters the fish-tailed beauty on Easter Eve. And before you scoff at the legend, let me tell

STRANGE BOULDERS NEAR CROWDEN TOWER

THE MYSTERIOUS MERMAID'S POOL ON KINDER'S WESTERN FLANKS

LOUIS J. JENNINGS, RAMBLES AMONG THE HILLS IN THE PEAK OF DERBYSHIRE (1880)

Kinderscout is regarded as strictly private property, and... is divided up among numerous holders, almost all of whom are at loggerheads with each other and with the public. The mountain – for one may so speak of it, seeing that it is close upon 2,000 feet in height – is one vast moor, intersected with long, broad patches of wet moss, and pools of dark water.

you the story of Aaron Ashton of nearby Hayfield, who was a regular visitor to the pool on the appointed day, and who lived to the patriarchal age of 104, dying in 1834.

These western slopes of Kinder were used by Mrs Humphry Ward as the setting for her melodramatic though little-read, Victorian novel *The History of David Grieve*. She describes: *"a magnificent curving front of moor, the steep sides of it crowned with black edges and cliffs of grit, the outline of the south-western end sweeping finely up on the right to a purple peak, the king of all the moorland round."*

*I*n physical terms, Kinder Scout is a 15-square-mile plateau of peat bogs, hags and groughs ringed by a sparkling diadem of gritstone tors which would not have seemed out of place in the studio of Henry Moore. In truth, the only places that Kinder remotely resembles Dr. Johnson's definition of a sharply-pointed hill is when it sends out one of its shapely courtiers, like Fairbrook Naze as seen from the Snake Road or Ringing Roger from Golden Clough, to tempt those who seek an audience with the mucky monarch.

The name itself is a bit of a puzzle. Like many of our most prominent physical features, such as most of our rivers and hills, it has a very ancient provenance. Prof. Keith Cameron assumed that was of pre-English origin, but confessed that there was insufficient material for adequate etymology. Certainly the 'Scout' element comes from the Old Norse *scuti*, meaning an over-hanging rock, and Eilert Ekwall thought it was probable that the first element came from the British *Cunetio* and the Welsh *briga*,

THE PENNINE WAY CROSSES THE TOP OF THE DOWNFALL

meaning hill. Others have assumed it to come
from the Saxon *Kyndwr Scut* meaning 'water over
the edge,' which is a pretty accurate description
of Kinder Downfall in spate.

The First Edition Ordnance Survey map
of 1864 clearly uses the name Kinder Scout to
describe the nick in the western face of the
mountain where the water falls – while the bulk
of the mountain is emphatically misnamed
'The Peak.' One of the earliest and most famous
clubs formed by walkers and climbers in the
surrounding cities in 1900 adopted the name
and became known as the Kyndwr Club.

As with many mountains, it had been
given different names by the folk who lived on
either side of it. So the illustrative map which
accompanied Michael Drayton's *Poly-Olbion*
of 1612 names the neat little molehill described
as rising above the source of the River Noe in
Edale simply as 'Nowstoole Hill.'

THE KINDER RIVER AT KINDER GATES

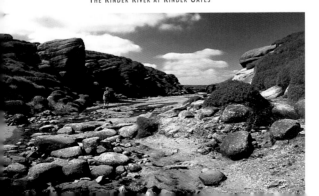

THE CELEBRATED "BLOW-BACK" AT KINDER DOWNFALL DURING HIGH WINDS

EDWARD BRADBURY AT KINDER DOWNFALL IN ALL ABOUT DERBYSHIRE (1884)

Looking up at the plunging water... a revelation of romantic beauty; the picturesque pushed to almost a theatrical point of possibility. The roar of the water fighting against the huge flanking rocks is the only sound. The sun catches the water, and now there is a dazzling constellation of diamonds; now there is a softer lambent light, as the shadow of an obtruding rock softens the glitter; then the spray is a beautiful prism; anon the smoke is a sunny mist broken into glints and splinters of light.

Stories of first-time visitors who, like me all those years ago, seriously underestimate the modest 2,088ft (636m) summit of Kinder are legend. You'll still hear them in the snug at the Old Nag's Head at Edale; tales of immaculately-equipped Pennine Wayfarers setting out from the village bright and early only to return bedraggled and completely disorientated the same evening, believing themselves to be at the next stop of Crowden-in-Longdendale. I've even seen a smartly-dressed couple blithely setting off up the Pennine Way in Grindsbrook carrying a suitcase in each hand. *"Going far?"* I asked incredulously. *"All the way,"* they replied.

Many ramblers only know Kinder as the first gruelling stage of Tom Stephenson's Pennine Way. But how many know that the hidden agenda for that great access campaigner's 30-year fight to set up the granddad of long distance footpaths was to open up the then-forbidden moorlands of Kinder and neighbouring Bleaklow?

LOOKING DOWN TO THE WATERY EYE OF KINDER RESERVIOR

THE UNFREQUENTED NORTHERN EDGE OF KINDER, OVERLOOKING ASHOP CLOUGH

EWAN MACCOLL, THE MANCHESTER RAMBLER (1932)
So I'll walk where I will over mountain and hill
And I'll lie where the bracken is deep; I belong to the mountains, the clear running streams
Where the grey rocks rise rugged and steep.

KINDER BECOMES A SEMI-ARTIC WILDERNESS IN WINTER AT CROWDEN TOWER

One of my most treasured memories of Kinder is when I walked with Tom, my hero and mentor, up through Grindsbrook Meadows in the mid-70s. It was just when the first horrors of so-called 'human erosion,' in the form of a six-lane highway were exercising the minds of countryside managers. Tom's views were revealing. Looking down at the path, he flashed that impish grin and said: *"It's no more ugly than the hags, groughs or screes of Kinder. It's as natural as a sheep track and, when all's said and done, I wanted the path to be used."* I often wonder what Tom would have thought of the flagged pavement which now winds up through the meadows and across Kinder's shoulders, or the floated geotextile mats which now take his 'long green trail' up England's backbone to Kirk Yetholm.

The other reason, of course, why Kinder occupies a unique place in rambling folklore is because it was the scene during 1932 of the fabled 'Battle of Kinder Scout,' when five deliberate trespassers were imprisoned for riotous assembly (see p83). That much-celebrated incident which at first divided, then united the access movement, is now widely acknowledged as an important catalyst in the whole access to the countryside

ERNEST A. BAKER, MOORS, CRAGS AND CAVES OF THE HIGH PEAK (1903)
Kinder Scout in winter is as wild a place as any mountain in England or Wales. To cross it is no less of an adventure than to cross Scawfell under like conditions, and the grandeur of and novelty of the experience repay one quite as well.

and national parks movement which culminated in the passing of the 'Right to Roam' Act in 2000.

Yet Tom Stephenson would never accept this. He often said the best thing to come from the whole event was Ewan MacColl's celebrated walkers' anthem, *The Manchester Rambler*, and he acknowledged that the lyrics could only have been written by a fellow bogtrotting trespasser:

"I've sun-bathed on Kinder, been burned to a cinder.

"And many more things I could tell."

For those generations of walkers whom MacColl immortalised as 'ramblers from Manchester way,' Kinder Scout was the nearest thing to a wilderness they could get for a sixpenny bus ride. But of course, wilderness is as much a state of mind as a physical reality. I once took a party of visitors from various American National Parks up Grindsbrook to show them the restoration work on the old Pennine Way, and one of them remarked: *"Hey, I thought you said you didn't have any wildernesses in your National Parks?"*

*T*o really know Kinder, you must see it in all seasons. When the Kinder plateau is white-over under a crisp blanket of winter snow, it is transformed into a semi-Arctic wilderness

sharing it's latitude with Siberia and Labrador. Walking across the plateau in these conditions is one of the great joys of the Peak. Then those ankle-sucking bogs between the hags and groughs, famously described by John Derry as *"the most featureless, disconsolate, bog-quaking, ink-oozing moor you ever saw"* are frozen firm underfoot, and surprisingly fast times can be achieved in the crossing.

During the long, hard winter of 1978, I struggled with a photographer friend through thigh-deep snow to witness the rare sight of Kinder Downfall frozen into a 100-foot-high curtain of sparkling ice. We had our lunch in the translucent light of the cave which had been formed behind the scintillating ice chandeliers, and then

EASY WALKING ON KINDER PLATEAU WHEN THE BOGS ARE FROZEN

watched spellbound as the climber who'd shared our picnic site took off, front-pointing up the vertical ice with crampons and ice-axe.

We were suitably impressed, but being mere walkers, we declined to follow his example and set off down to inspect the frozen Mermaid's Pool on the small plateau above the skeletal trees of Peter Nook Wood. We didn't see old Aaron's mermaid, but we did half expect to encounter Eskimo Nell, because we came across the bizarre sight of an igloo, perfectly-constructed from snowblocks cut from the frozen snowfield which surrounded the tarn.

At the other extreme of the seasons, Kinder can sometimes resemble a desert more closely than anywhere else I know in Britain's hills. Sean Jennett described it thus: *"The surface of the plateau of Kinder Scout is a desert in the absolute sense, for nothing grows here, not a blade of grass, not a tuft of heather, not a cushion of bilberry, and, as far as I am aware, not even moss or lichen."*

This is especially true of the area around Kinder Low, where even the peat has been eroded away by centuries of overgrazing, wind and

THE BOXING GLOVE STONES ON KINDER'S NORTHERN EDGE

rain to leave a Sahara-like expanse of receding peat banks and drifts of sparkling, silica-rich sand between the low, generally flat gritstone tors. It's humbling to pick up some of these grains of gritty sand and realise that as they are washed down into the cloughs and streams which drain the plateau and out into the river estuaries which feed either the North or Irish Sea on this watershed of England, they will eventually be compressed again to form the rocks of tomorrow's world – and start the timeless process described in the next chapter, all over again.

Another factor which has denuded Kinder of its peat blanket is fire, whether started deliberately as part of a heather management programme or accidentally by lightning strike or a thoughtlessly stubbed-out cigarette. Once a fire takes hold in the peat – which after all is a primitive form of coal – it can spread underground and burn for weeks, destroying a habitat which has taken thousands of years to form. The prominent 'bald patch' on the southern flanks of Kinder near Upper Moor is tangible evidence of a major uncontrolled fire in 1947.

*K*inder Scout has been described as one of the most walked-on mountains in Britain, and it is certainly one of the most popular. For many people, including me, it was their first taste of real wilderness, and will therefore always occupy a special place in our mountaineering memories.

Ernest Baker, author of the seminal *Moors, Crags and Caves of the High Peak,* was a pioneer turn-of-the-century trespasser on Kinder's bleak plateau, and he expressed its peculiar, esoteric charms perfectly:

"There is one characteristic of Kinder Scout which I think is quite unique in these islands. Sometimes when standing in the centre of the plateau, under favourable conditions, with the horizon falling on every side, and no ground within our vision higher than the curving lines of the moor immediately around us, one experiences that exhilarating sense of being actually on the roof of the world more vividly than when standing on the summit of a high peak."

It's that moment when the magic of Kinder Scout takes hold, and offers a sense of solitude and established stillness, older than the world. Can anyone hear music?

Adapted from Roly Smith's essay
"The Kinder Caper" in A Sense of Place
(Michael Joseph, 1998)

The Rocks Beneath

GEOLOGY BY DR TREVOR D.FORD

ICE IS STILL SCULPTING KINDER. ASHOP CLOUGH IN WINTER

GRITSTONE TOR ON ASHOP EDGE LOOKING TOWARDS FAIRBROOK NAZE

THOMAS L. TUDOR, THE HIGH PEAK TO SHERWOOD (nd)

The edges give by far the most thrilling sensations, and if you have ankles of steel so much the better for getting along through
their savage confusion. Perhaps the most superb viewpoint is Fairbrook Naze, and the edge of the Fairbrook waterfall.
But the region of the Downfall has, in itself, a wild beauty that excels all other places on the actual top.

*S*tanding on the high plateau of Kinder Scout, some 2,000 feet (600m) above sea level today, shivering in a biting wind, it is difficult to visualise the changes in geography which have taken place since the underlying rocks were formed. Those rocks tell us an intriguing story of a massive delta which built out into a sea characterised by limestone reefs and lagoons further south. Together they provide the contrasting Dark and White Peaks of the Peak District.

Roughly 300 million years ago, in what is known as the Carboniferous period of geological time, what was to become Kinder Scout was part of an enormous delta where a river was discharging its load of sediment into an ancient sea. Some of the grains of sand and scattered pebbles in the gritstones can be matched with their parent outcrops in the Scottish Highlands.

A river system comparable with the present day Mississippi gathered its waters from tributaries draining a range of mountains stretching from the Highlands to Scandinavia. It flowed southwards into a sea lying across the present site of the Pennines where it built out a delta like that around New Orleans today.

Britain then lay astride the Equator, enjoying a tropical climate, so the great river's banks and the delta-top had a cover of lush vegetation. Britain, in common with several of the Earth's crustal plates, has been drifting slowly northwards since Carboniferous times – 50 degrees north in 300 million years. In another 200 million years, we will be astride the North Pole!

To understand how geologists arrive at this story it is necessary to look at the rocks in more detail. The strata which make up Kinder Scout can be divided into five units displayed from the plateau downwards: *Kinderscout Grit; Grindslow Shales; Shale Grit; Mam Tor Sandstones,* and *Edale Shales.*

Collectively these total some 2,000 feet (600m) in thickness and they represent stages in the building out of the delta into a sea of that depth. When a river's velocity is slowed by meeting standing water in the sea, its carrying capacity is reduced and its load of sediment is gradually dropped. The coarse fraction, coarse sand and small pebbles, is dropped first nearest to the shore while the fine-grained mud washes out furthest. This settles on to the sea floor as much as up to 60 miles (100 km) offshore.

Very slow accumulation of mud yielded

A WINTER VIEW OF THE MOAT STONE, WOOLPACKS

the 1,000 feet (300 m) or so of *Edale Shales* which now outcrop in the floor of Edale at the base of Kinder Scout. Shells of marine organisms such as goniatites (extinct equivalents of the modern-day nautilus) and a variety of molluscs (equivalents of modern scallops and mussels) dropped into the sea-floor mud and survive as fossils today, usually squashed flat.

Hidden beneath the Edale Shales is *Carboniferous Limestone* which rises southwards to reach the surface around Castleton. In the 1930s it was thought that the limestone might contain oil resources and wells were drilled on either

side of Kinder Scout in Edale and near Alport. No oil was found but investigations continue and oil might yet be found one day.

As the delta grew out in to the sea, fine and medium grained sand were spread along the coast in the area nearest to the shore. These sands built an unstable mound-like mass along the shore which slumped from time to time yielding a turbid mass of sediment and water, cascading down the outer slope of the delta. As each turbid mass slowed down, it too dropped the coarsest material first and followed it with more silty sediment. Each couplet was probably

no more than three feet (1m) or so in thickness
but repeated turbidity currents resulted in an apron
of sediment fans at the foot of the main delta.

Around 500 feet (150 m) thick, they are
known as the *Mam Tor Sandstones.* Best seen in
the landslip scars of Mam Tor and Grindslow Knoll,
they contain many shiny flakes of mica, derived
from the schistose rocks of the Highlands, as well
as many fragments of carbonized plant material,
relics of the former vegetation cover upstream.
Each turbid flow tended to scour small hollows in
the underlying surface and the succeeding sand
filled them in yielding elongated sausage-shaped
lumps on the under-side of the sandy beds
known as flute-casts.

The *Shale Grit* followed and represents
a series of fans of fine to medium-grained sand
deposited on the middle slopes of the delta. The
name Shale Grit is rather inappropriate as there are
more sandstones than shale; the sandstones make
a distinct bench on the middle slopes of Kinder
Scout. The fans migrated according to the changes
in the pattern of distributary channels splaying out
across the delta top and turbidite channels down
its slope. Thicker and more blocky than the
Mam Tor Sandstones, the sandstones of the Shale
Grit can be seen high on Grindslow Knoll and in

the landslip scar of Back Tor, south of Edale. They
are widespread on the middle slopes of Kinder
Scout above Hayfield, along the Ashop Valley and
on the middle slopes of Win Hill.

The succeeding *Grindslow Shales* are really
rather fine-grained silts and sands deposited in the
slack areas between the main distributaries of
the delta. Though sandy rather than shaley,
with many mica flakes, they tend to split easily
and have the thin slabby appearance of poor-grade
flagstones. They are often concealed beneath
the fallen blocks below the plateau edge.

Finally, the *Kinder Scout Grit* is a sheet
of coarse sandstone with scattered pebbles which
represents the infilling of the sea close to
a migrating coastline. The great river had a

THIN LAYERS OF SHALE IN THE GRINDSBROOK GORGE

THE LAYERED, SEDIMENTARY CHARACTER OF THE KINDER GRITS IS WELL
SHOWN IN THE UPPER GRINDSBROOK GORGE

many miles across the southern and central
Pennines, the delta took a long time, perhaps a
million years, to build out in the way we see today.
A study of the inclined or current-bedding within
the gritstones permits the deduction of the
direction of current flow, dominantly from north
to south, confirming the general picture of a river
system draining the Scottish Highlands. A few
of the cliffs show cross-sections through infilled
and abandoned channels.

All of the above sandstones have
scattered fossilized relics of tree-trunks, branches
and roots. Rarely well-preserved, they are
samples of the thick tree-cover which lay on top
of the delta and across the hinterland upstream.
Doubtless there was an understorey of lower
vegetation of fern-like plants but they are rarely
preserved. Occasionally there are dimples on
bed surfaces, particularly the so-called Grindslow
Shales, left by the activities of burrowing
molluscs and worms.

At the end of the Kinder Scout Grit delta,
there were movements of the Earth's crust, and
the whole Pennine region subsided, so that
the process of building out a delta started again.
This gave us the *Chatsworth Grit*, well displayed in
Stanage Edge to the east and in Ramshaw Rocks

number of distributary channels like the modern
Mississippi, and the pattern of these changed
according to intermittent floods coming down
from the source area. Such floods may indicate a
seasonal, monsoon climate.

As the Kinder Scout Grit can be traced for

and the Roaches to the west.

A cycle of subsidence and delta-building followed, culminating in the *Coal Measures* of the Lancashire and Yorkshire coalfields. In the latter, long periods of swamp-like conditions on the delta-top allowed continued growth of lush vegetation which later compacted to form peat. In turn this was progressively compacted to yield the many coal seams.

It may be difficult to visualise, but all the strata of the later Millstone Grit and the Coal Measures once extended right over the present site of Kinder Scout, so that our original delta was buried to a depth of around $1^{1}/4$ miles (2km). It was the heat and pressure at this depth which converted the loose sediments of the delta to the cemented sandstones and shales we see today. At that depth of burial elevated temperatures well over 100 degrees catalyzed the dissolution of some particles in the pore-waters. Following chemical reactions, the materials were redeposited as cement holding the sands together and converting it to sandstone.

Some 10 million years later, at the end of

SOME TORS ARE STILL FORMING — EDALE ROCKS ABOVE JACOB'S LADDER

THE MOAT STONE AMONG THE WOOLPACKS

the Carboniferous period, there were great upheavals in the Earth's crust known to geologists as the Variscan Orogeny, and these resulted in the arching up of the Pennine Range to form an upfold or anticline about 155 miles (250 km) long, 62 miles (100 km) wide and at least 1 1/4 miles (2 km) high. Erosion set in and the highest parts of the upfold were progressively removed. With renewed upwards movement at intervals until some 10 million years ago, the original Kinder Scout delta was eventually uncovered.

Kinder Scout lies on the flat top of the arch so the strata are horizontal, but to the west, the strata tilt down beneath the Lancashire coalfield and an escarpment of the Kinder Scout Grit faces uphill either side of Hayfield. The strata here are inclined at about 15 degrees to the west. In Win Hill and Bamford and Stanage Edges, the arching effect is less severe and the grit is inclined at only five degrees.

The 290 million years since the Carboniferous era have seen further episodes of burial by younger strata alternating with phases of erosion which have removed all evidence of the younger cover. Its presence can be inferred from adjacent areas to both west and east and from the hardened condition of the rocks themselves. The last 10 million years have seen the trimming of the landscape by erosion as is discussed in the next section.

The landscape of Kinder. Shaped by Water, Wind and Ice

The science of the form of the landscape is called geomorphology. It includes a study of the attacks by the agents of erosion – water, wind and ice – and the landforms which result. What we see today is but a brief glimpse of how far an on-going combination of processes has proceeded in the total removal of Kinder Scout.

Water is the main agent, falling as rain or snow. Some percolates into the rocks to re-appear as springs lower down; some runs off as streams which merge to form rivers; some is used by plant growth, and some evaporates. It is the streams and springs which concern us most. Percolation water dissolves minerals in the rocks, re-emerging as springs carrying materials solution without our being aware of it. Run-off picks up loose particles as sediment. Soil and sub-soil are washed off adjacent slopes and carried downstream. As streams merge their carrying capacity increases and so does their erosive power.

The deeply-incised cloughs of Crowden Brook, Grinds Brook, and Oller Brook are the products of the steep stream courses carrying off eroded rock material. Boulders are trundled along, particularly in floods, and smash into each other, yielding sand and pebbles. The streams carrying these erode their beds and undercut their banks. Look at any stream in flood conditions and see how much sediment it is carrying.

Streams and rivers have eroded their valleys all round Kinder Scout. Tributaries of the River Derwent include the Noe and the Ashop. They have given us the Vale of Edale to the south and the Ashop Valley to the north, both joining the Derwent and discharging into the North Sea. The Kinder River and other streams drain through Hayfield to join the Goyt and eventually the Mersey which discharges into the

LOOKING TOWARDS ASHOP EDGE

THE WEATHERING PROCESS GOES ON AS WINTER TAKES ITS GRIP ON THE KINDER PLATEAU

LOUIS J. JENNINGS, RAMBLES AMONG THE HILLS IN THE PEAK OF DERBYSHIRE (1880)
*If I had to be cast adrift somewhere on a dark or foggy night, there are few places
which I should not prefer to the Kinderscout.*

Irish Sea. Kinder Scout is thus part of England's main watershed.

The rivers around Kinder Scout have all eroded their valleys to depths of 1300-1600 feet (400-500 m) below the plateau, perhaps taking anywhere from two to ten million years in an intermittent process related to the climatic changes of the Ice Age. The rivers will continue to widen and deepen their valleys until Kinder Scout is all removed. Estimates of the rate of erosion vary widely but at least 10,000 tons is taken away from Kinder Scout annually. There is a long way to go before it is all planed off!

Water also causes movement by lubricating *landslides*. Percolating rainwater tends to seep out as a line of springs at the base of the sandstones removing. The emerging pore water carries rock material in solution weakening the rocks and so sapping the support of overlying layers. While the largest landslips are on the Mam Tor side of Edale, their are smaller ones on the face of Grindslow Knoll, at the head of Grinds Brook and at Edale Head. Parts of the slopes below Kinder Downfall are an ill-defined group of merged landslips. Dating the landslips is difficult but some can be demonstrated to have been moving for at least 3,000 years. At least one, in

SAND-BLASTED TORS, SCULPTURED BY THE WIND ON KINDERS EDGE

the Ashop Valley, has been on the move for
8,000 years. On a much smaller scale, *soil creep*
is lubricated by rainwater, causing the terracettes
popularly known as sheep-walks. *Rock falls* are a
form of landslip and many slopes below the plateau
edge are mantled with blockfields, sometimes
known as clitter. Cluther Rocks on the western
escarpment are a good example.

Wind is best known as an agent of
erosion in desert country but it plays its part on
Kinder Scout by picking up loose sand-grains
and blasting upstanding rocks. Wind-blasted rocks
can assume some odd shapes such as the tors
known as the Woolpacks, Seal Stones on
Seal Edge and Madwoman's Stones further east.
Such tors are the result of a combination of
weathering by water which rots the rock down
joints, rainwash removing loose material and wind-
blast trimming providing a final trim to the shape.
The tors are the surviving cores of formerly

much larger rock masses in which the sandstone
is more firmly cemented.

Less obvious is the result of wind-blast over
the whole plateau at the time of the last Ice Age
when there was no vegetation cover, and rock
particles eroded from almost the whole surface
were spread far and wide by the Arctic gales.
The dust tended to settle further away to form the
silty clay known as *loess*. Much of the limestone
country south of Castleton is mantled by a metre
or so of such loessic material, now seen as a
yellow-brown silty subsoil. It is easy to recognise
here as it contrasts with the underlying limestone
but the same loess is hard to distinguish from
the closely similar underlying parent rock on the
Millstone Grit country.

Ice formerly covered much of Britain.
In the last million years Britain has been the scene
of at least four Ice Ages, perhaps as many as ten.
In each glaciation ice accumulated in the Scottish
Highlands, in the Lake District and North Wales.
Glaciers spread southwards, in some cases as
far as London. The main flow of the glaciers was
down either side of the Pennines, through
Lancashire into Cheshire on one side, and down
the Vale of York on the other. Ice accumulated

PREVIOUS PAGE: MOORE TORS — THE ANIMAL-LIKE SHAPES OF THE WOOLPACKS ON KINDER'S SOUTHERN SLOPES on top of the Pennines perhaps a half a mile (1km) thick, but it was held stagnant there by the flowing glaciers on each side and caused only minor erosion, so none of the valleys around Kinder Scout have developed the classic U-shape. There are no real corries, though some claims have been made that the hollows at the head of Seal and Blackden Cloughs might be poorly developed ones. If so, the glaciers they held were no more than 650 or 1,000 feet (200 or 300m) long and not sufficiently energetic to erode out fully-developed corries like those of the

Lake District and Snowdonia.

Thus Kinder Scout was covered several times by ice caps, though with little or no movement to bring material in, none of the caps left any boulder clay. The last such ice-cap was probably about 100,000 years ago, and the most recent glacial phase, ending around 12,000 years ago, had no ice-cap on Kinder Scout and the climate would have been that of a very cold tundra.

The tundra conditions of the last glacial phase, some 10,000-20,000 years ago, resulted in frozen ground or *permafrost*, well-known in

WATER AND ICE IN BLACKDEN BROOK

HAGS AND GROUGHS ON KINDERS NORTHERN EDGE

through the head and most show sections of gravelly mud deposits in their banks. The mantle is commonly about 10 feet (3m) thick but can reach 30 feet (10m). In the 10,000 years since the end of the Ice Age, the permafrost has all melted but the sludge is still slowly moving downhill towards the rivers yielding lumpy ground on the medium slopes.

In between the cold phases of the Ice Age the climate returned to normal and river erosion continued, but no landforms or deposits from these interglacial periods have been recognised around Kinder Scout.

The cover of *peat* is one of the notable features of the Pennine moors, and Kinder Scout is no exception. Most of the plateau has six or 10 feet (2-3m) of peat mostly composed of partly rotted sphagnum moss and heather. It contains pollen which can provide dates for changes in plant growth and these indicate a phase of lush vegetation in a slightly warmer period than now, between 8,000 and 6,500 years ago about 6,000-4,500 B.C. Cooler conditions ensued and peat growth slowed to a minimum, before erosion set in. In the last 2,000 years or so higher rainfall has caused the sodden peat to burst at the edges and gulleys have been eroded back

Arctic areas today. Each summer the upper layers melted to form a sludge of ground-up rock and fragments. On slopes the sludge moved downhill under a process known as solifluction. Sheets of solifluction deposits (often known as 'head') mantle the middle and lower slopes all round Kinder Scout. Stream gulleys have been eroded

LOUIS J.JENNINGS, RAMBLES AMONG THE HILLS IN THE PEAK OF DERBYSHIRE (1880)

At the top of the mountain, the walking is far more difficult than on the sides. Now begin the deep trenches, the long winding watercourses with sandy bottoms, the dangerous holes, thinly covered over with heather, the green oases in this sterile lane, which the traveller will touch only to his sorrow and dismay. You go along a yard or two and come to a yawning ditch, with no water perhaps at the bottom, but with soft peat sides which will scarcely bear your wieght.

to yield a meandering stream pattern.

Peat digging, walkers' feet, heather-burning, drainage channels and grazing have accentuated gulley formation until there is a network over the whole plateau. Many of the gulleys have been cut right through to the gritstone bedrock, often breaking up to white sand. Over-grazing and atmospheric pollution since the Industrial Revolution has killed some of the vegetation and bared large areas of peat so that gulleys have been eroded still further. Today's acid rain also accelerates the process of peat erosion.

Man's activities have also had some effect on the Kinder Scout landscape. Apart from peat digging and trampling, the escarpment has been the site of limited quarrying. This has been constrained by the difficult terrain and the haulage problems in bringing the dressed stone down to the roads and villages. However, there was some millstone production in small quarries on the western slopes, and some stone was also quarried for building reservoirs.

Kinder Scout itself provides important water catchment areas for Ladybower Reservoir in the Ashop-Derwent Valley and for the Kinder Reservoir above Hayfield.

As erosion continues, the landscape of

Kinder Scout will evolve still further. The removal of the peat cover is easily foreseeable. Some of the landslips are moving. The products of rock-weathering are carried away with each flood, which also erodes the river banks and beds. The ultimate result, long after present lifetimes, will be the levelling of Kinder Scout and its delta to sea level. But who knows what geological processes will interfere with that erosion, giving us a brand new landscape in the future?

KINDER'S MILLSTONE GRIT WAS QUARRIED FOR MILLSTONES, AS THIS ABANDONED STONE ON THE WESTERN SLOPES PROVES.

Birds and Bogs

NATURAL HISTORY BY STEPHEN TROTTER

THE DISTINCTIVE FLUFFY WHITE HEADS OF COTTON GRASS

THE PEREGRINE FALCON IS NOW INCREASINGLY SEEN OVER KINDER

EWAN MACCOLL, JOURNEYMAN (1990)

An elemental world of rock and sky, the wind and water, a world of mountains worn down to the bone long before the Alps or Himalayas were formed. A world where curlew, redshank and black-faced sheep were at home, where hawks, kestrels and rough legged buzzards quartered the sky in search of hares, voles and adders.

$\mathcal{T}$he dark and brooding Kinder massif stands at the foot of the Pennine Chain, a long tongue of relatively wild and untamed terrain probing south towards the lowlands of England. The wildlife of Kinder has much more in common with the hills and distant mountains of the north and west beyond than it does with the gentler surrounding lowlands.

Five significant habitats make up the moorland on Kinder:

- Upland heath with heather, bilberry and crowberry.
- Scattered wet 'flushes' and valley bogs on the lower flanks.
- Acidic grasslands on the flanks, edges and cloughs.
- Bracken in the drier areas.
- Blanket peat bog on the plateau and flat tops.

Occasionally there are also small remnant woodlands and isolated trees on lower slopes.

Wildlife of the upland heaths, wet flushes and acid grasslands

The moorland experience on Kinder is not just about spectacular views, gritstone tors and heather. In spring the whole character of the moors is transformed by the return of scores of birds to their nesting and breeding grounds. They spread far and wide over the moors and are attracted by the open habitats, the low numbers of potential predators and the supply of food.

Virtually every moorland bird species has a distinctive voice. Their calls, which define territory and courtship, are most evocative and stir emotion in even the most hard-bitten walker: the bubbling calls of curlew; the plaintive and melancholy whistles of golden plover and the flourishing shrill song of meadow pipits; the distant 'cronk' of the raven, not forgetting the unique 'go-back, go-back, go-back' of year-round resident, the red grouse.

The mix of birds is very special. Many are

THE RING OUZEL IS A DENIZEN OF KINDER'S CLOUGHS

THE HEATHER FADES IN LATE SUMMER IN FAIRBROOK

on insects and berries. They can often be seen gorging on ripe bilberry and rowan berries, but the reason for their decline is not yet fully understood.

The vegetation cover on Kinder is relatively natural and the distribution of plants depends on factors such as soil type, wetness and topography. Superimposed on this are the human effects of variations in grazing and burning.

Some parts of Kinder which have been traditionally managed for grouse and where numbers of sheep have been low are covered in heather moorland. There are surely no more impressive sights in the countryside than that of a heather moor in full bloom. During the hot, lazy days of August and September, the moors of Black Ashop, Nether Moor and Leygatehead seemingly come to life in an intense overload of the senses: changing from dark and moody browny-greens to startling pinks and shocking purples. The atmosphere is heavy with the scent of heather flowers and buzzing with the feverish activity of insects collecting the brief but abundant flow of nectar.

Where there have been higher numbers of sheep, the moors have lost much of their heather. These areas are often easy to spot as the widespread sandy-yellow hillsides which skirt

scarce and have decreasing populations such as the attractive ring ouzel. This shy bird is also known as the mountain blackbird, and is a relative of the common blackbird of our gardens. Unlike its cousin, ring ouzels spend the winter in North Africa. They inhabit the steep and open rocky slopes of many cloughs on Kinder, feeding

MRS. HUMPHREY WARD, THE HISTORY OF DAVID GRIEVE.
Some distance away in front of him, beyond the undulating heather ground at his feet, rose a magnificent curving front of moor, the steep sides of it crowned with black edges and cliffs of grit, the outline of the south-western end sweeping finely up on the right to a purple peak, the king of all the moorland round.

Kinder in winter. This acidic grassland is frequently dominated by mat grass – a tough, persistent and unpalatable grass which the sheep eat only when other, tastier alternatives have disappeared. In contrast, bilberry edges are thought to have developed where grazing levels are not so high.

Moors with dwarf-shrubs like heather, bilberry, cowberry or crowberry tend to have much more interest for wildlife than the grassy 'white' moors. This is because they are often structurally varied, offering more niches for animals to inhabit and providing good feeding opportunities for moorland species. Certainly many more birds are associated with shrubby areas, although only red grouse exclusively depend on heather.

Heather provides good nesting cover for rare birds like merlin, our smallest bird of prey, and short-eared owl, whose numbers fluctuate in response to the cyclical populations of their food, short-tailed field voles. In recent years both the merlin and short-eared owl have done well.

One of the other animals for which

THE RED GROUSE — MASTER OF THE MOORS — AMONG THE HEATHER OF ITS NATURAL HABITAT

SEEN IN ITS WINTER-WHITE COAT, THE MOUNTAIN HARE BLENDS IN WITH THE BACKGROUND

LOUIS J.JENNINGS, RAMBLES AMONG THE HILLS IN THE PEAK OF DERBYSHIRE (1880)

If the Kinderscout range were in Switzerland, scores of books would have been written about it, and 'Sanatoria' without number would have been established on its hillsides. As it is, not a dozen tourists throughly explore the Peak in the course of as many years, and the very people at the local inns which are nearest to it – and they are all some miles distant – seem to know little or nothing about it.

Kinder's moors are of interest is the mountain or blue hare. Adapted to the long and snow bound winters of the far north, this delightful hare was introduced to the Peak in the 19th century for sporting purposes. Heather management also provides all of its requirements which are remarkably similar to the red grouse: lots of young nutritious shoots provided by burning, with adjacent deeper shrubs in which to take shelter and cover from potential predators.

This is especially important here because of their tendency to grow a bluish-white coat for the winter – perfect camouflage perhaps for a Scottish winter, but not so effective in the milder climate of the Peak District. A good place to see them is in winter among boulder fields like those found at Cluther Rocks.

By far the richest diversity of plants is found in the wet moorland flushes where springs deliver a constant supply of clean groundwater to the surface. This is in contrast to the open moors where centuries of burning has eliminated all but a few tolerant species.

Here there can be an impressive mixture of plants ranging from, among others, mosses, rushes and the grass-like sedges through to exciting and attractive herbs such as bog violet, cranberry,

A MALE EMPEROR MOTH RESTS ON HEATHER DISPLAYING HIS SPECTACULAR WINGS

opposite-leaved golden saxifrage, bog asphodel, lesser spearwort and carnivorous rarities like the round-leaved sundew and butterwort. One or two of the best flushes also have populations of heath spotted orchids – a rarity in these parts.

The undisturbed flushes are also rich in insect life and many moorland birds bring their chicks to them in late May and June to gorge on the abundance of food. Some like the snipe spend virtually all of their summer in cover within these wet patches. One interesting introduction is the small colony of greater butterwort with their striking purple blooms on a wet rock outcrop in Grindsbrook, which has apparently survived since the 19th century. The ledges and rock outcrops within the cloughs are also often rich sanctuaries for plants, beyond the reach of nibbling sheep.

Invertebrates are an often overlooked element of our wildlife heritage – but nevertheless they play a critical role in the moorland ecosystem: pollinating flowers, recycling nutrients and feeding the birds. Some 250 species have been recorded on the western side of Kinder – by far the biggest group of animals with many local and scarce species. Mostly they pass unnoticed to visitors except perhaps when they are bitten by a midge or when they make a chance encounter with the striking beauty of an emperor moth, or the captivatingly-hairy and colourful northern eggar moth caterpillar slowly crossing a path on its progress to the next juicy-green bilberry leaf. Both of these moths are unusual in that the adults are active during the day. The females find a prominent perch from which to waft a chemical scent to attract potential mates from a wide area of the surrounding moorland: eggars do this during the late morning and emperors in mid-afternoon.

Open water is a less common habitat although there are a few shallow pools and ponds. Probably the best known is the magical Mermaid's Pool below the Downfall. This pool, formed in the bowl of a natural hollow, is slowly filling in as the adjacent peat bog grows – though it'll probably be many thousands of years before the process is complete. It's an excellent place to see cranberry and a variety of insect-life, such as an unusual bog pool spider. A number of dragonflies, including the black darter and the common hawker, are on the wing on calm, warm days in late summer.

In contrast, we have a love-hate relationship with bracken, a vigorous fern which in places is reasonably dense and abundant. Though it is poisonous and a headache for sheep farmers, bracken does have some value for wildlife. More than 40 types of insect are associated with bracken beds – as are a number of birds of conservation interest such as the ring ouzel, whinchat and twite. No-one can doubt its beauty in autumn when the fronds turn golden brown.

Wildlife of the blanket bogs

By comparison to the lower moorlands, the bogs of the plateau are a degraded and impoverished habitat – and all the more fascinating because of this. There are few other habitats in the British Isles that are quite as degraded or have as few species as the Kinder plateau. Nevertheless these are important places for species of conservation interest, as a major sink for carbon and for their historical interest – buried within the peat are pollen grains which record past environments of the area.

GORSE IN FLOWER IN JAGGER'S CLOUGH, LOOKING WEST

BILBERRY CLUMPS DOMINATE IN THIS VIEW OF THE BLEAK NORTHERN EDGE OF KINDER

J.B.Firth in Highways and Byways in Derbyshire (1908)

*Here are there great boulders stand up on the summit, jagging the sky line, and at intervals along the steep precipitous sides
there are clefts from top to bottom, some so deep as to resemble chasms with bare sides and courses for torrents in their stony beds.
The whole vast ridge, whose wonderful beauty of outline and form and mass contrasts delightfully with the moody moors,
was ablaze with yellows and greens, harmoniously blended to make the lovliest carpet for the hillside...*

A RARE TARN ON KINDER – THIS ONE IS JUST BELOW GRINDSLOW KNOLL

If the Kinder bogs were in good condition they would be intact and flat, with the water table near the surface, and have a carpet of sphagnum mosses. As any bogtrotter will testify, the reality of Kinder is far from this ideal: a network of groughs drain the peats, sphagnum no longer grows on the plateau, and huge areas of bare peat lie in a state of advanced erosion. Where there is a protective cover of vegetation the peat is possibly still accumulating but where it is bare, the peat is eroding.

Some erosion may have natural origins but there is no doubt that humans have caused the majority of the damage and this has accelerated in recent centuries. The deep peat is very fragile at this altitude and any disturbance to the surface layers can result in rapid erosion. Disturbance on Kinder includes pollution, widespread and uncontrolled fire, overgrazing and, to a lesser extent, trampling by people.

The bare peat is not an easy place for plants to grow. It is highly acidic and contains few nutrients. During the summer it becomes bone-dry as the network of groughs has lowered the water table. It is prone to washout after heavy rainfall and in winter deep frosts cause the

LOUIS JENNINGS, RAMBLES AMONG THE HILLS (1880)
The mountain – for one may so speak of it, seeing that it is close on 2,000 feet in height – is one vast moor, intersected with long, broad gulches, and abounding in deep holes, patches of wet moss, and pools of dark water.

surface to heave, breaking up any shallow roots – no wonder that few plants can survive, let alone recolonise, bare ground. Many of the wet bog species whose presence might be expected are therefore missing or very rare.

Only a handful of higher plants can tolerate these extreme conditions. They include heather, wavy hair grass, crowberry and bilberry. The commonest plants are the two types of cotton grass – the hare's tail and common cotton grass. The former is a long-lived sedge which tolerates the conditions and persists in tussocks for up to 100 years. It is easily spotted in fruit by

THE RARE, WHITE-FLOWERED CLOUDBERRY, THRIVING ON A KINDER PEAT BOG

THE RAVEN IS ONCE AGAIN BEING HEARD ON KINDER'S HEIGHTS

the single 'cotton ball' on the end of a stalk.

The common cotton grass has a different lifestyle. It does not form tussocks but spreads by underground rhizomes and is capable of rapidly colonising bare peat in the right conditions with an interconnected patchwork of roots which binds the peat together. It does quickly exhaust nutrients and often patches will die back at their centre after a few years. It is easily distinguished by the multiple white 'cotton wool' balls at fruiting.

One less common species of the peat is the patch-forming cloudberry – the bog 'blackberry.' This has one or two lime-green leaves which erupt during June into large white flowers that occasionally produce edible berries. On Kinder, cloudberry, like the ring ouzel and golden plover, is a species right at the southern end of its range.

Typical clough habitat — Golden Clough, with Ringing Roger in the background

Recently a rare shrub, bog rosemary, has been rediscovered on the Featherbed Ridge just north of Kinder. These isolated plants are probably a remnant of wetter times and fewer sheep and are just clinging on for the time being. Perhaps it may still be present out there on the plateau along with other possible rarities like the Labrador tea.

Yet again some of the bird life is of great interest. In addition to the red grouse, the Kinder plateau supports good numbers of another special species – the golden plover. This is an attractive wader with, as the name suggests, golden speckled plumage and a black chest. They show a strong preference for blanket bogs especially where dominated by cotton grass with some bare peat.

In recent years our understanding of its behaviour has improved greatly. The adults share the parenting effort and, amazingly, neither parent feeds on the moor. Instead they take it in turns to visit nearby in-bye pastures to feed – the males at night and females during the day.

The chicks' main diet is insects, especially daddy-long legs, which can be abundant. The birds appear to time egg-hatching with the peak emergence of these insects in late May – early June. The curious attraction of plovers with areas of eroded peat seems to be because the chicks find it easier to catch prey on bare peat rather than in thick vegetation.

So that's the natural aspect of Kinder: a wild place sustaining a very special wildlife heritage. Situated on the doorstep of millions of people in the great industrial towns of England, Kinder offers the chance to enjoy and experience at first hand a relatively wild moorland environment, abounding with some thrilling and spectacular wildlife.

GUARDIAN OF THE MOORS — THE SPANGLE-PLUMED GOLDEN PLOVER

A Mountain of Time

HUMAN HISTORY BY BILL BEVAN

LOOKING ACROSS GRINDSBROOK TOWARDS GOLDEN CLOUGH, SHOWING THE SLED ROADS USED FOR TAKING PEAT OFF THE MOOR

THE SOUTHERN SLOPES OF KINDER FROM LOSE HILL, WITH NETHER BOOTH (LEFT) AND LADY BOOTH CLOUGH (CENTRE)

JOHN LEYLAND, THE PEAK OF DERBYSHIRE (1891)
Although fine views of the pastoral valley may be had from the escarpments of Kinder Scout, they are much finer from the southern ridge, where, in the prospect, the escarpments themselves add wonderful variety to the landscape.

*K*inder Scout has long dominated the skyline of the study of the Mesolithic period, which followed the last Ice Age between 8,000 and 4,000 BC. Since the 19th century, numerous flint and chert tools have been found in eroded peat, so contributing important evidence to the understanding of Mesolithic people, not only on Kinder, but in Britain as a whole.

This in many ways is the start of the known history of the human relationship with Kinder which continues to the present day. The succession of generations who have lived, worked or travelled across Kinder over these millennia had different ways of organising their societies and of perceiving the land, and through time it is their interactions with its rocks, soil and vegetation that have shaped the mountain we know today.

From Ice Age to Iron Age

Analysis of ancient pollen preserved in peat bogs has shown that at the end of the last Ice Age, the vegetation of the Dark Peak comprised alpine species, such as dwarf birch, juniper and buttercup. This was soon replaced after the retreat of the glaciers by an influx of other species forming thick forests from the valley bottoms to the lower moorland plateau. Above 1,640ft (500m), there was a more open mix of birch and hazel scrub with alpine plants.

Numerous finds of stone tools show that people lived on the uplands and in the valleys during the Mesolithic and early Neolithic periods. These people were mobile, travelling around the landscape and settling temporarily at different locations to gain access to a variety of resources such as plants, game, timber and water, or to hold gatherings and ceremonies.

The majority of the high-altitude sites on Kinder could represent temporary camps which were occupied during short-term food gathering trips. Such movement across the landscape would have been based on a complex set of rights negotiated between different families and communities, perhaps invoking ancestors or memory to justify the occupation of specific locations at certain times.

For the majority of the year, it is likely that different families had relatively little contact

ENCLOSURE FIELDS BELOW GRINDSLOW KNOLL SHOWING THE CHANGING BOUNDARY OF THE INTAKE LAND

with each other, perhaps seeing other groups while hunting or coming across the cold fires of previous occupations. At times, gatherings would be held where land-use rights could be negotiated, goods such as flint exchanged, prophecies foretold and ceremonies celebrated. During the Neolithic period, large chambered tombs and henges were built for ancestral rites and ceremonies, however the closest to Kinder were on the limestone plateau, suggesting people travelled long distances for big gatherings.

Peat had already begun to spread on the higher moorlands after the Ice Age but was halted by woodland, especially by the denser forest on the lower moors. It is thought that people used fire to make clearings to attract large game animals, such as deer, to more abundant vegetation. The repeated burning of vegetation is suggested by the concentrated finds of carbon and charcoal in virtually every pollen sample dating from this period.

While forest clearance was a sustainable strategy in lowland areas where woodland regenerated easily, this was not so in uplands such as the Kinder plateau, where nutrients were washed out of the soils once the tree cover was broken. This coincided with a wetter climate

and open areas eventually became waterlogged so that peat reached today's limits during the early Neolithic period.

As this peat formed, people continued to be mobile, the contrast between the wooded valleys and the open moorlands providing different resource opportunities. Sherds of pottery and flint tools have been found dating from the later Neolithic period, but in much smaller numbers than previously. This suggests that Kinder was less intensively used after peat had formed, while settlement continued in the surrounding valleys as finds in the Upper Derwent valley show.

Dramatic evidence for the strong ties still held with the mountain are the earliest built structures to survive. Between approximately 2,500 to 1,500 BC, at least four burial barrows were built on the massif to mark the location of the dead. They are all deliberately placed on prominent points overlooking valleys, so making the burial places of the dead highly visible from the surrounding area, even at distances where the barrows themselves can not be seen.

Barrows help to remind the living of their ancestry, of their kinship with their community and of their association with a geographic location. Not everyone was buried in a barrow, instead they were built when the community felt the need to reassert its links with the land and its ancestors through a funeral ceremony.

Situated near Tunstead Clough are the likely remains of an ancient settlement, possibly later prehistoric or Roman. There are two oval platforms here where round or oval buildings once stood. We know little about settlement in the Dark Peak during this period. People may have become more settled in the valleys, increased their cultivation of cereals and used the moors for summer pasture and quarrying. An Iron Age or Roman corn-grinding quernstone was found among Cluther Rocks in 1969.

From Medieval to Modern

During the Anglo-Saxon and Early Medieval periods, the region may have been part of the domain belonging to a semi-autonomous group known as the *Pecsaetna* 'Dwellers of the Peak' who were recorded in the 7th century.

The area is then first named in the Domesday survey of 1086, where Hayfield and Kinder appear as parts of the King's own estate. This was the Royal Forest of the Peak, an area of land granted by William the Conqueror to William Peveril in 1068, which included much

ABANDONED ENCLOSURE WALLS ON GRINDSLOW KNOLL, LOSE HILL IN THE BACKGROUND

ERNEST A. BAKER, MOORS CRAGS AND CAVES OF THE HIGH PEAK (1903)

As I skirted the crags, ness after ness jutted out from the long, mountainous escarpment into the golden haze that shut out the world;
and, in the deep bays and coves between, late fields of snow gleamed in the shadow and glistened in the sun.
The russet hues and ruddy gold of the grass patches covered the fell-side with warm colour...

IMPROVED MEADOWS AND MOORLAND BEYOND FROM THE SNAKE ROAD

of the Dark Peak west of the River Derwent and the limestone area between Tideswell, the River Wye and the Goyt Valley. Peveril Castle at Castleton was the administrative centre and the Foresters' Chamber was at Peak Forest. The term 'forest' does not necessarily imply the existence of woodland, and much of the Peak Forest at this time was not. Forest was a Norman word to describe a royal hunting reserve, many of which were imposed across England by the conquerors.

Forest management often differed from the law and could actually be susceptible to greater landscape change than land outside forests. Grubbing out woodlands, enclosing land or building settlements may have been forbidden by law, but it was often allowed in return for an annual payment known as a fine. The opportunities for new settlement and enclosure within forests were actually greater than outside because there was less existing settlement

and Forest Law was used as a way of generating revenue for the Crown.

It is likely that at least some of the farmsteads in the valleys surrounding Kinder were established during this period as they were in the Upper Derwent. By the 16th century the amount of settlement had grown so much that land began to be taken out of Forest Law until the Forest was finally abolished in 1674.

Parts of Kinder were reputedly also monastic estates during the Medieval period. Basingwerk Abbey in Flintshire had lands to the north, forming an estate centred on Glossop and Charlesworth, while Merevale Abbey in Warwickshire held lands to the east, as well as in Chinley. Edale Cross is thought by some to have been a boundary marker for Merevale's estate.

The cross is the only definite Medieval feature on Kinder. It has traces of Saxon-style knotwork which suggests that it was originally carved before the Norman Conquest, though it also has later Medieval decoration and is inscribed with the date 1610 next to the initials JG. This is likely to be the mark of John Gell, a 17th century road surveyor. As well as a monastic boundary marker, the cross has being interpreted variously as a guidestone for the adjacent

ETHEL BASSETT GALLIMORE, THE PRIDE OF THE PEAK (1926)

Like to some kingly monster of the primels Kinder, black unwieldy, fenced and strong;
His sleepy cloughs towards the fastness climb, and oozy ridges lines his plateau long.
The mist comes hurling high o'er Edale cross, and sheep upon the benty bastions graze,
And swiftly falls the dreadful dark across, the far ferocious rind of Fairbrook Naze.

Hayfield to Edale packhorse route, a boundary marker for the medieval parishes of Hope and Glossop, and the point where three wards of the Royal Forest of the Peak met. It is likely that these boundaries were actually based on each other, later boundaries following earlier ones.

Today most of the mountain lies within these three parishes – Hayfield, Edale and Hope Woodlands, with the cross situated between Hayfield and Edale. On the east are two other possible medieval structures, Hope Cross and the remains of Woodlands Chapel, associated with the Glossop to Hope packhorse route.

From Commons To Privatisation

From the Medieval period onwards, the high moor was predominantly open common land on which tenants had rights to pasture livestock, cut peat and quarry stone. Small-scale stoneworking was carried out on outcrops and boulders across much of the common to produce door steps, lintels and troughs.

On a larger scale, millstones were produced in the boulder field of Cluther Rocks where many

EDALE CROSS – THE FINEST MEDIEVAL LANDMARK ON KINDER

ABANDONED MILLSTONE ON KINDER'S WESTERN SLOPES ABOVE HAYFIELD

imported from Cologne and northern France due to political upheavals in northern Europe.

This does not mean that this was the only period that the millstones were made here. The industry may have started as early as the 14th century and only died out by the 19th century.

Other, stranger, examples of stone-working include the Dog Stone and Charge Stone. The former lies among the millstone quarries and is inscribed, in code, with the lines *"She may be green but she is of the best green stone."* The latter, the Charge Stone, is on Sandy Heys and was charged with energy for use by a group known as the Aetherus Society during the 20th century.

Ruined walls and lines of cairns can still be seen on the moor. These were built to mark the boundaries of different peoples rights on the common rather than to enclose land as such and to aid stock management.

The rights and routines of using the common land meant that tenants not only had an important resource but also defined their identities through the connection with it. Each of the surrounding farms had their own sheep pastures, known as heafs, on the higher moors with cattle pastures and peat cuts on

small quarries, abandoned millstones and small shelters can still be found. A map of 1640 shows this area as a millstone quarry, complete with tiny drawings of millstones and it names the stream as Milne Stone Brook. This date is contemporary with the height of millstone production in Britain, when high quality millstones could not be the lower shelves and stone-built sheepwashes in the cloughs.

The limits of some peat cuts can still be seen as straight vertical edges cut into the blanket bog. Wooden sleds were used to bring down the peat to the farms, gouging sinuous routes into the valley-sides, such as the holloway still known as the Sled Road, running down the valley of Grindsbrook into Edale. These can be made out above the enclosed farmland when low light casts long shadows. Peat stopped being used as a fuel in the 19th century when the new turnpike roads and railways allowed cheap coal to be imported.

Prior to the building of the turnpikes, or toll roads, packhorse routes were the main long-distance rights of way with their origins in the Medieval period. Kinder is crossed by one packhorse route which connected Hayfield and Edale via Edale Head.

Trains of up to 40 or 50 packhorses walking in single file would have been a common sight on this route. The earliest record of the route is in 1290 when it is referred to as *"le Cauce"* which suggests that it was a raised causeway, though there is no evidence today for this surviving. It was later known as the Monks Road because it was reputedly used by the

monks of either Merivale or Basingwerk Abbeys who had been given land in the area.

Lying between the farmland of the surrounding valleys and the open moor are areas called intakes. Tenants had progressively enclosed and improved land above their farmland, known as 'taking-in,' hence the name 'intake' for such enclosures. This was carried out over a long time sometimes by agreement between tenants and landowners, though it could also be a way for

A RECONSTRUCTION OF A JAGGER AND PACKHORSE AT EDALE

THE REMAINS OF A SHOOTERS' CABIN IN ASHOP CLOUGH

tenants to exert dominance over their landlords by increasing tenure over land. Some of these intakes are now part of the improved farmland while others were not sustainable and fell out of use, their walls now lying ruined and the land reverted to moorland.

Then in 1836, a traumatic change to land-

use of the common occurred in Hayfield parish when the Parliamentary Act of Enclosure was passed. The major landowners put forward the Act to take the land out of common use, in effect privatising the land so that it could be rented at a higher price. This quashed the historical rights to pasture, peat cutting and stone quarrying so restricting these activities to the farmers who rented or bought the land.

Luke Garside, writing in *Kinder Scout – the Footpaths and Bridleways about Hayfield* (1880) said that most of Kinder had been 'King's Land' over which there was free public access. But he tabulated the award of acres after the 1830s enclosures:

> "To the rich, according to their riches –
> 2,000 acres.
> To the poor, according to their poverty –
> 0 acres."

The enclosures also imposed a new, rigid, scheme of ruler-straight walls onto the landscape such as those on either side of Oaken Clough and west of Kinder Low. These walls can be seen on the maps of the area, in stark contrast to the more organic shapes of the older fields in the valleys.

Enclosure also allowed landowners to develop grouse shooting by limiting the numbers of sheep so that the newly-created gamekeepers could manage the moors for grouse breeding. In many ways this echoed the Forest Laws imposed by the Normans during the Medieval period.

However this time there was another group of people willing to protest against such authoritarian control – the walkers and ramblers of the surrounding towns and cities. The archaeology and history of rights of way became an important weapon in the ramblers' fight for access to moorland, as demonstrated by G.H.B. Ward in the Sheffield Clarion Ramblers'

handbooks and the work of the Peak and Northern Footpaths Society.

Archaeology shows that Kinder as we know it today, in all its apparent bleakness and wilderness, has been shaped by millennia of human use since the last Ice Age. Even the blanket peat which characterises the mountain's landscape today was as much the result of the action of people as the climate.

THE RECONSTRUCTED PACKHORSE ROUTE OF JACOB'S LADDER

Forgive us our Trespassers

ACCESS HISTORY BY ROLY SMITH

TRESPASSERS ASCEND A KINDER CLOUGH IN THE 1930s

THE SCENE OF THE TRESPASS IN THE UPPER REACHES OF WILLIAM CLOUGH, LOOKING SOUTH TOWARDS THE KINDER RESERVOIR

JOHN DERRY, ACROSS THE DERBYSHIRE MOORS (1904)

Nothing keeps alive the spirit of revolt and iconoclasm so fiercely as a refusal to the general community of the use of their eyes over beautiful remote tracts of earth, under the plea of private ownership. The rocks of twenty thousand years echo laughter at the arrogance of the claim: "These are mine and no other men may even pass near and look at them."

*S*unday, April 24, 1932 dawned fine and clear: a perfect day for enjoying that away-from-it-all, top-of-the-world feeling uniquely and so easily available to ramblers on the high moorland of Kinder Scout.

But 70 years ago, the highest and wildest moorland of the Peak remained frustratingly out of bounds to the growing army of walkers who had joined the huge rambling craze in the surrounding cities. Only a dozen footpaths of two miles or more crossed the open moorland of the Peak District, and not one crossed the 15 square miles of the ramblers' Holy Grail, the 2,000-foot summit of the Kinder Scout plateau.

Unlike today, Britain was then 'bumping along the bottom' of the depths of an abysmal depression, and nothing that Ramsay MacDonald's Labour Government could do seemed to help. Dole queues stretched in the streets of Manchester and Sheffield, and the newspapers were full of reports of demonstrations by the unemployed, as the jobless total topped three million.

The Great Escape offered by the misty, inviting moors of the Peak, just a sixpenny bus ride away from the grimy, back-to-back terraces, was a magnetic temptation; a chance to recreate in the true sense of the word. Many were prepared to risk an encounter with the burly gamekeepers who jealously guarded the moors for their grouse-shooting masters.

Trespassing had become a popular sport, adding an extra *frisson* of excitement to a moorland ramble. G.H.B.Ward, the King of the Sheffield Clarion Ramblers, had dubbed the pastime, "*the gentle art of trespass,*" and gained the dubious distinction in 1923 of having a writ served on him making him apologise for past trespasses on Kinder, and promise not to trespass again. "*But the gamekeepers are not always there,*" he gleefully reported in the 1952-53 Clarion Handbook, "*and after a while, the amount of general trespassing did not decrease.*" He regarded the writ as "*a greater honour than any OBE,*" and added: "*May Kinder be 'free' in 1953, and may those who never knew this fight for Liberty deserve the Victory by their use of, and behaviour on, Kinder Scout.*"

*I*t was against this kind of background that the famous Mass Trespass on Kinder Scout took place. There can be no doubt now that the trespass was politically motivated. But it was born out of a mounting sense of frustration felt by

DAILY DISPATCH, April 25, 1932. Price 1d.

Daily Di...

THE NATIONAL NEWSPAPER ...

MONDAY, APRIL 25, 19...

NO. 10,034. [REGISTERED AS A NEWSPAPER.]

MASS TRESPASS ARREST...

FREE FIGHT WI... GAMEKEEPERS ON MOUNTAI...

RAMBLERS HELD U... POLICE CORDON...

AMAZING SCENE... MOORLAND VILL...

LADY NUTTALL and party at the Cheshire Hunt Point-to-Point Races at Brindley Lea, near Nantwich, on Saturday.

AFTER a free fight on Kinder Scout, peak, between gamekeepers and a ramblers who had organised a mass day, a cordon of police was drawn across Hayfield to meet the ramblers returning t...

Six ramblers, all from the Manchest... taken into custody.

The mass trespass, in which about 4... ramblers took part, was organised by the Sports Federation, and was meant to be the vast tract of Kinder being closed to th...

The procession of ramblers set... out from Hayfield about 2 p.m. and moved along the path to William Clough singing military

HITLER'S NEW BID FOR POWER.

NAZIS LEADING IN ELECTIONS.

PRUSSIA'S POLL.

Berlin, Sunday.
...TEST returns of voting in
...elections,

TELL-TALE FILM OF CUP GOAL.

BALL OVER THE LINE.

WINNERS AT SEASIDE.

SERVIC...

atch

Ideas
and Town Talk
Brightest and Best of
the Week
EVERY SATURDAY · 2d.

ORTH.
BROADCASTING:
PENNY.
Page Three.

N KINDER SCOUT

A general view taken during the meeting held by ramblers at the foot of Kinder Scout yesterday.

FIRE RUINS FAMOUS CHURCH.

VALUABLE SCULPTURE DESTROYED.

VICAR AS FIRE FIGHTER.

From Our Correspondent.
Sunday.
nea

"Inheritance,"
the Novel of
the Year,
will start
in the
"Daily Dispatch"
TO~MORROW

400 A STS IN

TRIAL OF 31 CONVICTS.

PRINCETOWN ASSIZE THIS WEEK.

JUDGE TO STAY AT AN HOTEL.

ELABOR

many young outdoor people at the apparent lack
of progress made by the rambling establishment
towards the long-standing goal of obtaining
free access to Britain's mountains and moorland –
a goal now within sight after the recent passing
of the Countryside and Rights of Way Act.

Intellectuals like Prof. C.E.M.Joad
and Prof. G.M.Trevelyan appeared to support
the idea of trespass. Joad, addressing a ramblers'
rally in The Winnats, Castleton, had told his
audience: *"If you want the moors to be free, you must
free them for yourselves."* Most interpreted that as
an invitation to trespass, although Joad later
denied this.

The rambling federations of Manchester and
Sheffield were opposed to the use of direct action.
Both Harold Wild of the Manchester federation
and Stephen Morton of the Sheffield group went
on record as saying that they believed the trespass
had put back the access campaign by 20 years.
It came at a time when they genuinely believed
they were at last beginning to break the power of
the landowners by getting them to agree to
meet around the conference table.

Access campaigner Tom Stephenson,
while opposing the tactic of mass trespass, thought
this was nonsense. The cynical emasculation in

FREEDOM TO ROAM — WALKERS PASS THROUGH THE ONCE-FORBIDDEN GROUND OF THE WOOLPACKS

F.H. BRINDLEY, WRITING IN THE YORKSHIRE TELEGRAPH AND STAR, FRIDAY, 7TH MARCH 1930
ON KINDER SCOUT YESTERDAY. WHY IT IS UNSUITABLE FOR A NATIONAL PARK: A PLACE OF THRILLS AND DANGERS
'Rambler,' who writes in Monday's 'Star,' might have been a member of my own party who explored Kinder Scout
with a camera on behalf of the 'Star' yesterday, when we had adventures sufficient to last us for many years, and convincing
us that as a National Park we do not think Kinder Scout will fill the bill.

Parliament of the 1939 Creech Jones Access to Mountains Bill showed how little reasonable hope there was for access legislation at the time. Stephenson acknowledged that the 1932 Mass Trespass was the most dramatic incident in the long access campaign. *"Yet it contributed little, if anything, to it,"* he claimed. Edward Royce, access secretary of the Manchester federation and a leading champion of the access cause, was equally dismissive. *"The year 1932 will not be remembered as a red letter year for the rambler,"* he wrote soon afterwards. *"It has been a period of more than the usual froth and bubble."*

Royce's successor as access secretary was Philip Daley, later to become national chairman of the Ramblers' Association and chairman of the Access and Footpaths Committee of the Peak District National Park authority for 19 years. As such, he was closely involved in the negotiations for the first access agreements with the landowners in the Peak, and said he found the mass trespass was invariably used as an argument **against** public access. *"Such access as we have gained,"* he wrote, *"owes nothing whatever to the mass trespass... and I can say quite categorically without fear of contradiction that the mass*

MRS. HUMPHREY WARD, THE HISTORY OF DAVID GRIEVE.

In ordinary times the Downfall, as the natives call it, only makes itself visible on the mountain side as a black ravine of tossed and tumbled rocks. But there had been a late snowfall on the high plateau beyond, followed by heavy rain, and the swollen stream was today worthy of its grand setting of cliff and moor. On such occasions it becomes a landmark for all the country round, for the cotton spinning centres of New Mills and Stockport, as well as the grey and scattered farms...

trespass was a positive hinderance and deterrent to the discussion and negotiations to secure the freedom of the hills."

The idea of a mass trespass originated during the Easter 1932 weekend camp of the Communist-inspired British Workers' Sports Federation at Rowarth, on the western edge of Kinder Scout. A visiting group of London-based BWSF walkers had been turned back by abusive and threatening gamekeepers at Yellowslacks, on the western

THE LATE BENNY ROTHMAN, ON HIS WAY TO KINDER

'THE PICCADILLY CIRCUS' OF KINDER – THE DOWNFALL ON A BUSY WEEKEND

approach to Bleaklow from Glossop. Back at the campsite, it was agreed that if enough ramblers had been there, no number of keepers could have turned them back. *"We decided then and there to prove the point,"* recalled Benny Rothman, then secretary of the Lancashire district of the BWSF, who died at the age of 90 in January 2002.

*W*hich was why that sunny Sunday morning found Rothman, then a 20-year-old unemployed motor mechanic, and his best friend Woolfie Winnick, cycling out of Manchester to the friendly village of Hayfield, which shelters under the western ramparts of Kinder Scout. They were already wanted men, having used their bikes to avoid police waiting at Manchester's London Road

station with a restraining injunction against the event, which had been deliberately well-publicised by Rothman in the Manchester newspapers. The bells of St. Matthews Georgian parish church were ringing out as Benny and Woolfie planned the event which was to change the course of rambling history over a cup of tea in the village tearoom.

*W*hat happened next is now firmly established as part of rambling folklore. The march of about 400 ramblers from Hayfield Recreation Ground to Bowden Bridge quarry, (where a plaque unveiled on the 50th anniversary now commemorates the event); the impromptu speech by Rothman when the main speaker failed to arrive; the joyful, arm-in-arm, singing procession up the Kinder Road by Nab Brow above the reservoir and into William Clough; and the sudden break-out onto the forbidden ground of Sandy Heys at the pre-arranged signal of three blasts on Woolfie's whistle.

Tom Stephenson always insisted that the trespassers never reached the summit of Kinder Scout, which is two miles away and about 400 feet higher, and the available evidence seems to bear him out. Rothman himself said that the body of ramblers was about half-way up William Clough on the Hayfield to Snake Inn public footpath, which had been negotiated by the Hayfield and Kinder Scout Ancient Footpaths Association as long ago as 1897, when the trespass actually began.

At Woolfie's signal, they started to scramble up the steep slopes of Sandy Heys in open formation. A line of between 20 and 30 keepers was waiting for them on the brow of the hill. The few, undistinguished scuffles which followed resulted in one temporary keeper, Edward Beevers, being knocked to the ground, injuring an ankle.

Press photographs taken at the time actually show concerned ramblers coming to his assistance. John Watson, one of the group of stick-wielding keepers waiting on Sandy Heys said afterwards: *"We could hear them cheering and yelling as if they had achieved something, when they had achieved nothing at all. They had only trespassed about 100 yards – they never got halfway up the clough."*

Rothman later agreed with Stephenson that the so-called 'victory meeting,' when the Hayfield

THE PLAQUE IN BOWDEN BRIDGE QUARRY, UNVEILED ON THE 50TH ANNIVERSARY OF THE TRESPASS

THE TRESPASSERS MARCH BY THE SIDE OF KINDER RIVER TOWARDS KINDER SCOUT

group met up with others from Sheffield, who had come by the much more difficult route across Kinder's peaty plateau from Edale, was held near Ashop Head, at least two miles north-west of Kinder's hard-to-find summit. But in the end, what was more important was that they had trespassed in such a public and positive way, rather than how far they had trespassed.

The trespassers agreed that they would march back to Hayfield *"with their heads held high"* and not disperse like a band of criminals. *"It was a demonstration for the rights of ordinary people to walk on land stolen from them in earlier times,"* Rothman was to write later. "We were proud of our effort and proudly marched back the way we had come."

The police, who had declined to take part in the scramble up Kinder's steep flanks, were waiting in a line across Kinder Road when the trespassers returned. Five people were arrested, in addition to John Anderson, a rambler actually opposed to the trespass who had just come along to see what would happen, but was apparently arrested when he went to assist the injured Beevers. They were variously charged with public order offences such as riotous assembly, but significantly, not with trespass.

The story of the trial of the trespassers at Derby Assizes is as riddled with the same kind of class prejudice as the rest of the event. The judge, Sir Edward Acton, was true to the best traditions of English justice. When it was revealed that a copy of a book by Lenin had been found in the possession of one of the accused when arrested, he innocently enquired, to the merriment of the court: *"Isn't that the Russian gentleman?"*

Rothman's self-conducted defence, prepared in the darkness of a Leicester prison cell, was a masterpiece of open-air, working-class rhetoric. *"We ramblers, after a hard week's work in smoky towns and cities, go out rambling for relaxation, a breath of fresh air, a little sunshine,"* he told the court. *"But we find when we go out that the finest rambling country is closed to us, just because certain individuals wish to shoot for about ten days a year."*

Ironically, it was the severity of the sentences handed down by the judge on the five young

JUST LIKE THE OLD DAYS: A GROUP OF TRESPASSERS FROM 1932 MET UP WITH HORACE OLDHAM, A WATER BOARD BALIFF (LEFT) AGAIN IN 1970 DURING THE MAKING OF A BBC FILM. THEY WERE (RIGHT TO LEFT), EWAN MACCOLL (WRITER OF THE MANCHESTER RAMBLER); TONY GILLETT (IN THE BACKGROUND); BENNY ROTHMAN (CENTRE WITH RUCKSACK), AND DAVE NESBITT.

defendants – ranging between two and six months' imprisonment – which was to unite the ramblers' cause. Even those implacably opposed to the trespass were appalled by the 'savage' sentences, and the Manchester federation was among many who appealed to the Home Secretary for a remission. A writer in the *Manchester Guardian* compared the affair to a univeristy student rag, pointing out that people arrested during rags were not usually sent to prison. The Clarion Handbook of 1933-34, reported that the stiff sentences handed out *"did not bring laurels to the other side"* and thousands of ramblers were reported

to have gone to view the scene of the trespass immediately after the event.

The annual ramblers' access demonstration in The Winnats a few weeks later drew a record 10,000 people, and further mass trespasses followed at Abbey Brook in the Upper Derwent, and on Stanage Edge, but significantly, no arrests were made.

*I*ndisputably, the mass trespass on Kinder in 1932 bought the access issue to a head, and acted as an important catalyst to the whole National Parks and access to the countryside campaign which eventually led to legislation in 1949. When the Peak District National Park authority came into being in April 1951, it lost no time in addressing the access problem, and it was no accident that the first-ever access agreement allowing walkers the freedom to roam was signed just a year later, covering 5,780 acres of Kinder Scout and Broadlee Bank Tor. Today, more than 80 square miles of moorland are covered by such agreements.

The 'Right to Roam' Countryside and Rights of Way Act of 2000 can be seen as the crowning culmination of the efforts of those brave pioneering trespassers, though few will live to see its enactment. There can be little doubt either, that the Kinder trespass has entered the realms of the mythology of the outdoor movement, giving its few survivors a totally unsought aura of martyrdom.

FREEDOM FOR ALL — CELEBRATING THE 50TH ANNIVERSARY OF THE MASS TRESPASS AT THE HEAD OF WILLIAM CLOUGH

KINDER SCOUT TRESPASSES

£5 REWARD

will be paid for the name, address and occupation
of any of the persons represented in the photos.

Apply:— COBBETT, WHEELER & COBBETT, Solicitors,
49, Spring Gardens, Manchester.

The Bad Old Days

RECREATION BY ROGER REDFERN

Permit Mr A. L. Redfern
& party to visit the Downfall
on Sunday Nov 15th 1925 —

James Watts

J.T. Merritt
R Barn
S E Barn
W. Wall

Watts compliments

S. & J. WATTS & Co.
MANCHESTER.

Telegraphic Address "WATTSES"

It has been my practice of late to al[low]
members of the public, who asked for su[ch]
permission, to walk over my portion of Kind[er]
Scout, when I could do so without detriment [to]
the value of the ground as a grouse moor.

Were I, however, to accede habitually to the
ever-increasing number of such applications, the
moor would soon lose its entire sporting value.
The continual crossing of the ground is quite
enough to make the grouse—a most shy bird—
depart.

I trust, therefore, that those who apply will
not think me unreasonable if on account of the
breeding and shooting season, or for other
reasons connected with the proper management
of the ground, I am from time to time compelled
to refuse the desired permission.

JAMES WATTS.

A PERMIT ISSUED ISSUED TO ROGER REDFERN'S FATHER BY LANDOWNER JAMES WATTS FOR A VISIT THE DOWNFALL IN 1925

*U*p to the time of the sporting landowner, Kinder Scout was rarely crossed; its wild spaces were considered "uncanny and repellent." Local folk and travellers looked up at the high ground and were said to have "shivered even in midsummer."

When my father and his friend began walking on Kinder Scout immediately after the end of the Great War, they usually took the precaution of carrying with them a letter from James Watts, the landowner, giving them permission to cross the high ground. Watts was a Manchester wholesale warehouse owner and also a keen game sportsman.

In those days, these were major expeditions but my father had the advantage of staying from time to time with the Misses Champion at Grindslow House, just upstream of Grindsbrook Booth, Edale. In this way, as guests of the local landowners, they had the great advantage of legitimacy when they encountered farmers and gamekeepers.

On one occasion they took the risk of venturing onto Kinder Scout without current permission from Watts, and they were spotted near the Downfall and reported. My father promptly received a warning letter from Watts's solicitors demanding a written apology and 6s 8d (33p) to cover their charge. Wisely my father apologised and paid the fee.

In the autumn of 1925 my father applied to Watts as usual for permission to cross the western side of Kinder Scout and received in reply a printed notice pointing out that there were now so many requests for permission that the moor would *"soon lose its entire sporting value."*

WALKERS ENJOY THE VIEW FROM KINDER ACROSS EDALE TO LOSE HILL

ON KINDER'S NORTHERN EDGE

ALFRED WAINWRIGHT, PENNINE WAY COMPANION (1968)

*The attractions of the Kinder escarpment are unique. Along the edges the walking is dry and firm,
with little rise and fall, over terrain marked by weathered boulders and surfaced by sand and gravel, a natural terrace between
the naked peat of the plateau and the gritstone cliffs. One's appetite is whetted for more, and in fact there is
a recognised circuit of the Kinder Edges well worth walking.*

Though the notice continued that Watts hoped that *"those who apply will not think me unreasonable if I from time to time an compelled to refuse the desired permission,"* there was written on the reverse side: *"Permit Mr A.L. Redfern and party to visit the Downfall on Sunday, November 15th, 1925. James Watts."* The names of his four keepers were added and compliments given.

*L*ooking back over three quarters of a century, it is difficult to appreciate how devoid of human presence the highest point of the Peak District was. Leaving Edale and going up Grindsbrook Clough and right across the plateau to Kinder Gates and to the top of the Downfall, then returning by Fairbrook Naze and Seal Edge before crossing to the top of Grindsbrook, my father's party would not have seen a living soul except, occasionally, a gamekeeper striding the crest of the edges on the lookout for trespassers.

Even in the early Fifties, after the National Park had been established, it was quite an event to see another party of ramblers crossing the plateau or descending one of the major cloughs like Crowden or Fairbrook. In those halcyon days, of course, footpath erosion was virtually non-existent, the going underfoot much easier and route finding more of an adventure.

That 'King of Ramblers,' G.H.B.Ward of Sheffield, could rightly be called the pioneer of walking on and around Kinder Scout. With their first ramble right round the perimeter of Kinder Scout in 1900, Ward's Clarion Ramblers Club became the first bona fide hill walking group of consequence in Britain. What is perhaps surprising is that rock climbing had begun here almost a decade earlier.

Thanks to the Peak District and Northern Counties Footpath Preservation Society, the path connecting Hayfield and the Snake Inn became a public right of way for all time in 1897, but only after a long tussle. It was the Hayfield and Kinder Scout Ancient Footpaths Association which started the struggle for this path as early as 1876. The Snake Path was one of the very first public paths across truly wild country which wasn't an ancient bridleway, like the Jacob's Ladder-Edale Cross track linking Edale and Hayfield.

*T*he most popular way to the tabletop of Kinder Scout has always been up the sinuous valley of Grindsbrook Clough, as fine a mountain defile as any in the entire Peak District. The cone of Grindslow Knoll looks down from the west

on the ant-like forms of ramblers, balanced by the shattered cock's comb of Ringing Roger, high to the east. The path goes up steadily, passing shaly cliffs where natural oil oozes out to send shimmering rainbow hues across the plunge pools in the racing brook. The main clough eventually turns through a right angle towards the north and enters an impressive ravine, hemmed in by gritstone walls. In dry weather progress is interesting as you climb the rock steps carved out by the foaming brook over many centuries. Then, quite suddenly, you come out onto the open plateau surface and are faced with the seemingly endless undulations of the strange, tundra-like world you've just entered.

This route from Edale, up the length of Grindsbrook Clough and onto the top of the plateau, was the line followed by the Pennine Way, brainchild of Tom Stephenson, when created in 1965. The route then headed north-west directly to the top of the Downfall, but as the years went by and ever more walkers followed this popular long distance path, the erosion of the plateau surface became so bad that the original 'bad weather alternative' route was adopted as the official route. Today, the heavily-laden pilgrims setting out for the Scottish Border head

JOHN HILLABY, JOURNEY THROUGH BRITAIN (1968)

...fed up with the sight of peat, I took off my shoes and socks and climbed onto a crest of the soggy stuff. I didn't sink in far, but the prospect from the top was appalling. The peat extended for miles. It rose, gradually, in the direction of a mound of rocks. And it steamed, like manure. Manure is the analogy that comes most readily to mind. The top of Kinder Scout looks as if it's entirely covered in the droppings of dinosaurs.

due west from Edale, crossing the fields below
Broadlee Bank to Upper Booth and Jacob's Ladder
before turning north to skirt Kinder Low, before
re-joining the original route at the top of the
Downfall. The fragile botanical balance up near
the 2,000 feet (600 m) level is protected somewhat
from former pounding by paving, and Pennine
wayfarers get an easier first (or last) day crossing
to the Snake Pass, en route for Bleaklow and
Longdendale.

Beyond the Downfall the Pennine Way
skirts the top of dramatic broken ground above
Sandy Heys before dropping off the bold, north-
west pointing spur which is the westernmost point
of the entire plateau. A restored, paved path
takes you down to the head of William Clough to
cross the Snake Path before the gentle rise
to Mill Hill, where the route turns through
90 degrees to eventually cross the Snake Road
on its way to Bleaklow.

*U*ndoubtedly the finest expedition
on Kinder is the circuit following the edge of the
plateau, preferably in a clockwise direction
with the sun (if it's shining) generally behind you
all the way. A good starting point is the car park
off the Snake Road, just above the head of

the Ashop arm of Ladybower Reservoir. A stiff pull
up through the coniferous plantation gives
access to the Roman road near Crookstone Barn
from where you soon enter Open Country on the
westward ascent to Crookstone Out moor.

In clear weather it's a delightful progress
heading eastwards across the top of Jagger's
Clough to the rocky promontory of Ringing Roger,
then round the head of Golden Clough and
so across the tops of Nether Tor and Upper Tor

PLODDING THROUGH A KINDER "GROUGH"

CROSSING NETHER TOR ABOVE GRINDSBROOK

to come to the head of Grindsbrook Clough's rock-girt ravine.

Over the top of the moor, you next come to the top of Crowden Brook and, scrambling to the summit of Crowden Tower, you gaze over the wide sweep of the Vale of Edale towards Rushup Edge and Mam Tor. Not far to the west you traverse what must be the most remarkable collection of gritstone tors in all of Peakland. Walter Poucher called this fascinating assembly of natural erosion 'Whipsnade' because of the resemblance of so many tors to animals; but the Ordnance Survey calls them the Woolpacks, and they were certainly known as such locally as early as 1809, on account of their likeness to the large sacks of wool seen on the backs of pack horses.

Pym Chair and Noe Stool are two further distinctive tors which punctuate the skyline of Edale Head, before the circuit walker turns back to the north near Kinder Low's trig. point. Heading north towards the Downfall there are broad vistas out over Kinder Reservoir and beyond Hayfield towards the Cheshire Plain.

Heading eastwards you go right along the northern edge, known simply and unequivocally as The Edge to the bold prow of Fairbrook Naze, that commanding headland overlooking the plantations and interlocking spurs of Ashop Valley and beyond to the great sweep of Bleaklow. Next comes Seal Edge and Blackden Edge, with views into the beautiful Hope Woodlands and up the secret turnings of Oyster Clough and Alport Dale.

In the end you reach Crookstone Knoll, last spur-ending of the easternmost plateau. The far eminence of Derwent Edge blocks the north-eastern horizon, while Win Hill is a focal point to the south-east. The circuit of Kinder Scout is now complete; as fine a high level ramble as any in England, given clear weather, strong legs and lungs.

Kinder is now also the focus of a number of fell-running events, which test the mettle of runners throughout the year. Among the classics are the 25-mile Marsden-Edale and the 40-mile High Peak Marathon (also known as the Derwent Watershed), but others include the Kinder Trog, the Edale Fell Race and the Edale Skyline. All these are serious endurance events, demanding high levels of stamina and route-finding skills.

*A*s already mentioned, the pioneer rock climbers weren't slow to discover the delights of the gritstone outcrops on Kinder Scout, despite the problems of access. The first explorations seem to have taken place on on Nether Tor and Upper Tor – the crags overlooking Grindsbrook Clough – in 1891. It was J.W.Puttrell and W.J.Watson from Sheffield who created the Primitive Climb on Nether Tor and the Promontory Climb on neighbouring Upper Tor.

But by 1900, Puttrell and his friends were exploring the obvious challenges of the great buttresses near the Downfall and also along the northern edge above upper Ashop Clough. Kinder Great Buttress, south of the Downfall, has one of the best situations of all the gritstone crags. A big, exposed crag with wonderful vistas out to the west, it has some classic routes

FELL RUNNERS ON THE "CROOKSTONE CRASHOUT" TACKLE CROOKSTONE KNOLL

including the Very Severe, 300-foot (91m) Girdle Traverse.

Over on the northern side, The Edge has several areas sufficiently wide and steep to offer many routes. In 1901 Puttrell and friends made first ascents which include the 60-foot (18m) Ashop Climb and Hanging Chimney. Further east is the dramatically-sited Chinese Wall on Seal Edge, where the routes are short but steep and look out over the broad landscape towards Bleaklow.

*K*inder Scout sheds much of its water into the Downfall ravine, and during hard winters this high, exposed waterfall often freezes to produce an impressive hanging curtain of translucent green or blue ice which provides some of the best ice-climbing in the Peak.

The steep ice wall in its dramatic setting is an established favourite and has thrown down a challenge to winter climbers for the last hundred years. The annual tradition of climbing there was established by Fred Heardman, who made regular ascents in the years before the Second World War. That tradition has continued, although nowadays, the use of modern ice-climbing equipment in the form of short axes and

ZIGZAG CLIMB IN THE KINDER DOWNFALL AMPHITHEATRE

JOHN LEYLAND, THE PEAK OF DERBYSHIRE (1891)
...one may picture them (the great escarpments of Kinder Scout) as gigantic bastions and towers, broken and shattered at the top, where some Titanic conflict went on...

rigid crampons has reduced the difficulty. Despite this, an ascent of a frozen Kinder Downfall is still a must for aspiring winter mountaineers.

The 164 ft (50m) Downfall Climb is the most popular route up the icefall and starts up the right corner to a large platform followed by a leftwards traverse, then up a short vertical ice-wall or corner to finish. In good conditions the central ice pillar, with its cascade of icicles, can produce a very steep and serious climb. However, good ice is a rare commodity these days and, as soon as the Downfall freezes, the ravine often takes

ICE CLIMBING ON KINDER EDGE

on the appearance of a circus as groups of ice-climbers compete for an ascent of the frozen waterfall before it collapses into a pile of shattered ice splinters.

The rim of the Downfall ravine is lined with steep crags and those on the left flank usually contain ice runnels which provide short climbs where you can easily escape the crowds. To the right is the impressive Kinder Great Buttress, occupying what must be one of the most exposed positions of all gritstone crags. To the right of the steep rocks is Arpeggio Gully, a good introductory snow climb and over to the left side is the enigmatic Twopenny Tube, which sometimes gives an exciting winter ascent.

Elsewhere, some of Kinder's rocky cloughs, such as Crowden Clough, Blackden Clough and the right fork of Grindsbrook Clough, can sometimes provide long and exciting winter outings when the rocks and boulders in their upper sections are cloaked in ice and snow.

But in general terms, the crags on Kinder Scout are rather too remote for many modern rock athletes - they'd rather step straight from their car onto the foot of their crag. The long slog up Grindsbrook Clough or up William Clough from Hayfield is not to their liking. So you can often find these rock exposures quiet and much as Puttrell and Baker and Alf Bridge found them in the early part of the 20th century.

After all those years of tediously having to obtain permission to walk across Kinder (or run the risk of being caught without a permit), my father and I saw the funny side of an incident on a day soon after the plateau and its flanks became Open Country and subject to an Access Agreement negotiated by the National Park.

We were descending from Fairbrook Naze towards the Snake Road in wet and windy weather. Some distance ahead of us was a pair of ramblers. They stopped and looked back at us. Seeing my father's trilby hat and plus-fours, they had a hurried conversation then, turning, made off down the slope at good speed.

It was plain that they weren't aware that this part of Kinder Scout was now open to all and they obviously thought my father was a gamekeeper!

On the Edale skyline, looking towards Mam Tor (left) and Brown Knoll (right)

Looking After Kinder

MANAGEMENT BY STEPHEN TROTTER

GORDON "THE WARDEN" MILLER, NATIONAL PARK RANGER AT EDALE FOR OVER 30 YEARS, ON THE SLOPES OF THE NAB LOOKING TOWARDS GRINDSLOW KNOLL

THE UBIQUITOUS SHEEP — CREATORS OF THE KINDER LANDSCAPE.

*W*hen the National Trust acquired the Kinder Estate in 1982 it was, quite simply, being over-run by hungry sheep. Locals say that 'the grass is always sweeter in Kinder' and trespassers of the wooly kind were attracted from Edale, the Snake and elsewhere. More than 2,000 sheep could be grazing on the western edges of the moor at any one time – about two and half times the sustainable number.

The estate was widely recognised as being in an advanced state of degradation, with its wildlife interest and rugged beauty blighted by the impact of pollution, fires and overgrazing. The edges and slopes had become 'fragile ground' where patches of short grass clung to nearly bald hummocks, separated by unstable, bare and eroding ground. Dwarf shrubs, particularly heather, had disappeared and been replaced by

BLACKDEN BARNS, RESTORED BY THE NATIONAL TRUST, IN THE WOODLANDS VALLEY WITH KINDER BEHIND

EDWARD BRADBURY, ALL ABOUT DERBYSHIRE (1884)

The entranced eye skips over gray gritstone knoll and wild clough, lying immediately below, wine-stained in heather-bloom, and accentuated in outline in the white, cloudless light; passes the lonely white farmhouses that here and there give a human interest to the spacious solitudes in the slopes of the valleys; lingers for a moment on the soft peaceful repose of Edale and wanders over the map-like area of far-off peak and plain, now sharply defined in the impalpable silver haze of heat.

mat grass. With the degradation there had also been a decline in the numbers and presence of moorland birds and other wildlife, though some species which like open ground, like predatory beetles, were doing well. It was vital that sheep numbers were reduced.

Kinder, like other upland areas, had seen a rapid rise in the numbers of sheep, especially since the last war. Studies have shown that following the introduction of government subsidies the numbers of sheep have tripled in the parishes of Kinder, and as a result the amount of heather has declined by around 30 per cent.

An early survey of the Peak District by C.E. Moss in 1913 provided valuable evidence that the slopes of Kinder had once supported a typical moorland flora of mixed heather and bilberry. We also know that it had been managed as a grouse moor until just after the Second World War. Thus the Trust's initial management objectives for Kinder had a clear purpose:

- *to restore the diverse moorland vegetation.*
- *to reduce the erosion of fragile ground.*
- *to conserve the moorland's wildlife.*

The Trust immediately took the bold and pioneering step of banning sheep from Kinder. The grazing rights were neither let nor exercised, even though this was unpopular with some local farmers. This in itself was not sufficient because of the considerable levels of sheep trespass. The Trust therefore adopted a two-pronged approach:

- *to mend all the historical boundaries around Kinder (about six miles of wall and fence).*
- *to physically remove and then return "bandit" sheep to their owners.*

The Trust's wardens acquired sheepdogs and have regularly gathered Kinder ever since. In total, more than 38,000 sheep have now been removed in this way. By 1985, the grazing was under control and the resulting changes on the Kinder flanks have been documented by monitoring work.

The changes combined major reductions in the amount of bare ground with a dramatic increase in wavy hair grass and a slow but welcome return of heather and bilberry. There are now more than 185 acres (75 ha) of moor with a good proportion of dwarf shrubs and some

60 acres (25 ha) dominated by heather. Still a long way to go but encouraging nevertheless.

Broad Clough has seen the most change; it was the last area to lose its cover of heather – and the first to regain it. Heather is now spreading across and up the more exposed upper slopes. By 1993, the successful restoration had reached the stage that controlled burning could be carried out in Broad Clough for the first time in 40 years.

A recent Environmentally Sensitive Area Scheme requirement to create a large enclosure by renewing a traditional boundary has given us the opportunity for some controlled grazing with cattle on the southern slopes of Kinderlow End in Bennetts near Stoneyford. The light summertime grazing will create some open gaps in the grass for the establishment of more dwarf-shrubs.

The appearance of the moor is slowly reverting to one which Moss might recognise. The process is slow in this harsh environment and there is still some way to go before the restoration is complete across the whole of the western edge. Wildlife is already responding, since 1984 for example, the red grouse population has shown a

GATHERING SHEEP ON KINDER

LOOKING FROM THE NAB TOWARDS GRINDSLOW KNOLL SHOWING THE EXTENT OF THE 'INTAKE' LAND

JOHN LEYLAND, THE PEAK OF DERBYSHIRE (1891)
There are surely few more entrancing prospects of stern and lonely grandeur in these rugged hills than when the great escarpment glows in the light of the setting sun.

HEAD OF THE EDALE VALLEY FROM RUSHUP EDGE, WITH KINDER ON THE RIGHT, AND GRINDSLOW KNOLL FAR RIGHT

dramatic increase: from one pair to between 16-24 pairs within two monitoring areas.

Management of the lower moors

The unfenced Kinder massif stretches from the outskirts of Glossop in the west to Jaggers Clough and Edale in the east. There are nine 'hefted' flocks with something like 2,500 sheep grazing this area during the summer.

Hefting is the traditional way in which sheep are bred and shepherded to stay on a particular piece of hill without the need for fencing. It relies on the tendency for sheep to be loyal to the place which they were born. Ewes will, like racing pigeons, return and stay in more or less the same areas to give birth to their own lambs; with the hefting instinct passed on. But with the demise of regular shepherding in the Peak District, this often only partially works and some sheep still wander.

On the heather areas of Black Ashop and Nether Moor the red grouse is a free-range, entirely wild game bird, unique to the British Isles. Moorland management for grouse involves two key activities: burning narrow strips of heather in winter, and the legal control of predators like crows and foxes in order to maximise the yield of grouse in August.

The key to maintaining good moorland is the burning of old heather, which promotes growth of young, nutritious shoots on which the grouse feed. A mosaic of different aged patches is created by rotational burning on a cycle of around 8 -12 years. This is important as the birds also require adjacent areas of deep, 'leggy' heather in which to take shelter and nest. The strips are narrow because the strongly-territorial red grouse is reluctant to leave the security of cover for more than about 50 feet (15m), hence the strips should be no more than 100 feet (30m) wide. Keepers attempt to maximise the productivity of the moor by providing for all of a pair's requirements within a small area, so cramming in as many territories (and birds) as possible.

This mosaic of heather also benefits many other birds like merlin, short-eared owl and in places golden plover, whinchat, ring ouzel and lapwing.

Conservation of the Blanket Peat Bogs

The present condition and future of the blanket peat bogs up on the plateau is less rosy. Though some erosion may be natural, four complex environmental factors, dating back centuries, have been implicated in the greatly accelerated rate of peat erosion over the last 300 years. These are:

● *Atmospheric pollution from the cities which surround the southern Pennines. This has wiped out the sphagnum mosses from the plateau, opening the peat to erosion.*

● *The widespread occurance of uncontrolled fires especially in summer, which has removed extensive areas of vegetation and burned into the peat itself in many places.*

● *Overgrazing by sheep.*

● *Footpath damage and resulting erosion in some places.*

ONE OF BRITAIN'S TRUE DESERTS – THE FAST-ERODING PEAT AT KINDER LOW

SEAN JENNETT, DESERTS OF ENGLAND (1964)

The surface of the plateau of Kinder Scout is a desert in the absolute sense, for nothing grows here, not a blade of grass, not a tuft of heather, not a cushion of bilberry, and, as far as I am aware, not even moss or lichen. Immense brown hummocks of peat curve nakedly down to channels where water was worn its way to the stony foundation of the mountain – though water flows in the channels only after heavy rain.

TUSSOCK GRASS AND A FROZEN GROUGH ON BROWN KNOLL

The result is large areas of bare peat. Even since the mid-1970s some 74 acres (30ha) of vegetated peat have been lost, and on average erosion continues at an average rate of 25-50 mm (1-2 ins) per year.

The Trust's main objective has been to reverse this loss by minimising the damaging impacts on one hand, and by re-establishing plants on bare areas on the other. Peat which has a protective cover of vegetation is relatively stable and the underlying principle is that the best place for the peat is *in situ* on Kinder, and not in water courses or the nearby reservoirs, where it is very costly to remove from drinking water.

A great number of re-vegetation trials have been carried out, some with great success, others less so. The results have shown the need to:

● *Where possible raise water levels to wet the dry peat and in places, treat the effects of strongly acid peat by applying low doses of lime.*

● *Stabilise the mobile peat by sowing a nurse grass crop/spreading brash. However, shallow rooted grasses are susceptible to frost-heave and trampling. It is vital to also introduce more robust deep-rooted species like cotton grasses or heather which may become established in the temporary shelter of the nurse grasses.*

● *Introduce local seed and plant live transplants in bare areas e.g. by spreading heather seed and planting local turves of cotton grasses and bilberry with the use of small dams to keep the peat wet.*

● *Encourage any surviving plants to spread and seed by reducing the grazing level of sheep. Experience has shown that reducing grazing levels does work, though it takes a long time.*

One key problem is the preference of grazing animals for younger and presumably tastier shoots on the fringes of spreading patches. This slows any natural re-colonisation. The Trust and other landowners use these intensive approaches in two situations: for restoration of damaged ground beside footpaths, and on old fire sites such as Kinder Low and Ringing Roger.

One most welcome development for Kinder since 1989 has been the introduction of the Environmentally Sensitive Area scheme, a government backed initiative to help promote environmentally sensitive farming and management of the countryside to improve the landscape for wildlife – and for heather moorland in the North Peak. This has helped to fund a range of improvements, such as reductions in sheep numbers and various moorland restoraton projects. The successes are to be seen across the Kinder moorlands and have 'cut with the grain of work' which organisations like the National Trust have been undertaking.

Wild Fire

Fire is a massive threat on the peat moors of Kinder – and could well be the major cause of bare peat in some areas. Kinder Low is a significant 'hotspot' as many paths cross here. In the last 20 years there have been some dozen or so fires of varying size in the vicinity of the trig. point. Four massive fires occurred in this time: one in 1980 beside the Pennine Way above Sandy Heys, another between Kinder Low and Three Knolls, one around Red Brook and the other above Ringing Roger. None of these have fully recovered despite the best efforts of land managers. We now place great emphasis on preventing fire and then if they do occur, investing resources in specialised equipment to put them out as quickly as possible before they spread.

Even some of the most specialist 'go-anywhere' off-road vehicles can be defeated by the terrain on Kinder. Often the only fast and efficient means of delivering water to the fire

FIGHTING A FIRE IN THE PEAT ON KINDER

A MOORLAND FIRE IS DIFFICULT TO EXTINGUISH, AS PEAT WILL BURN UNDERGROUND FOR WEEKS

JOHN HILLABY, JOURNEY THROUGH BRITAIN (1968)
From the botanical point of view, they are examples of land at the end of its tether. All the life has been drained off or burnt out,
leaving behind only the acid peat. You can find nothing like them anywhere else in Europe.

HELICOPTERS ARE THE EASIEST WAY TO GET WATER TO REMOTE MOORLAND FIRES

is by helicopter. The costs of moorland fires can therefore be immense in terms of the time and effort required and in helicopter costs. However the environmental costs of not fighting these fires is even greater: the direct effect on wildlife and on the dirty water flowing into the reservoirs of Kinder and Ladybower in the catchment area.

Access and footpaths

The National Trust cares for most of the Kinder massif except for Grindsbrook and parts of Crowden Clough. As far as possible, the Trust attempts to pursue an integrated approach to the sustainable management of Kinder: trying to strike a balance between different land-uses and interests. This is important for the Trust as its aim is to look after the place forever, for everyone, whatever their background.

One vital aspect is to ensure that people can enjoy, experience and engage with the splendours of wild Kinder. It is important people get the maximum possible enjoyment from this marvellous hill so long as its done in a sustainable way.

The Trust strongly supports the freedom for people to roam on Kinder: the hill is open and will remain so forever (foot and mouth outbreaks permitting). Nevertheless, footpaths are key to the way most people enjoy and use open country. Research has shown that the vast majority of walkers use them on moorlands, not surprisingly, to get to their intended destinations. Their maintenance is therefore a vital activity to balance the needs of people and conservation so that the large numbers of visitors don't destroy the precious and fragile environment they've come to experience.

The trampling of vegetation and subsequent erosion of soils and peat by wind, water, boots and frost has become a common problem on many popular walking routes. A number of different repair techniques have successfully been used to provide sustainable surfaces in many upland areas of the UK including Kinder, these techniques are:

● *Stone pitching – a randomly stepped path built*

HELICOPTERS ARE ALSO USED TO TRANSPORT SLABS FOR FOOTPATH REPAIR

by carefully placing boulders and turf, a single route on sustainable surfaces is defined, allowing the by-passed redundant paths to revegetate. Some five miles of the path on the Kinder edges have been treated in this manner without the use of any imported or artificial surfacing material.

Flags have been used on routes on the ascent to Kinder Low around Swine's Back and on parts of the fringe path above Edale near the Pagoda. This technique has caused some controversy in recent years, although the paths are remarkably successful; people use them and they do blend in given time. The good news is that if fashions change and the flags are no longer used, then they will simply disappear as the cotton grasses grow over them and absorb them into the peat mass. The routes have been shown to dramatically reduce disturbance to birds such as golden

of large embedded stones – as used at Scout End, Jacob's Ladder and Kinder Low End.

● The use of stone flag surfaces to cross deep blanket mires in a revival of an old technique originally used by packhorse routes in the southern Pennines and Yorkshire.

● The use of realignment techniques where,

FOOTPATH EROSION ON THE PENNINE WAY AT ASHOP HEAD

plover and enable the recovery of damaged ground.

Note that most footpath schemes are not often intended to make access easier for the walker. However unless the finished path is comfortable, at least to a greater degree than the adjacent terrain, then the work will fail. It is also important that, as far as is reasonably possible, paths should be designed so that man-made features do not create unnecessary

REPAIRS UNDERWAY BY NATIONAL TRUST WORKERS AT ASHOP HEAD

barriers which may exclude some sections of society. There is often little that can be done with natural obstacles but nevertheless we have a duty to ensure that artificial works do not inadvertently prevent access for some groups.

The message from successful upland footpath work is that it is possible to have excellent access for visitors and conserve our precious and fragile habitats at the same time.

THE RESTORED PATH NEATLY PITCHED, WITH VEGETATION ALREADY RETURNING

What Future for Kinder?

CONCLUSION

BY ROLY SMITH & STEPHEN TROTTER

LOOKING TOWARDS THE KINDER PLATEAU FROM THE SNAKE PASS

ON THE EDGE OF KINDER PLATEAU

EDWARD BRADBURY, ALL ABOUT DERBYSHIRE (1884)

The moors have often been compared to the sea; and the vast breadth of undulating distance at Kinderscout gives special force to the trite fancy. It is an ocean of billowy heather; distant hills rise like dark sea cliffs; a far-off ordnance survey cairn supplies the illusion of a lighthouse; here and there a block of dark gritstone, growing above the purple waves, with the sun catching on its weather-stained side, conveys the suggestion of a russet sail; a remote farm looks like an island in the heathery sea.

*K*inder Scout means all things to all men. To walkers, it gives a unique sense of freedom, somewhere where, a short bus or train ride away from the surrounding cities, they can really feel they have got away from it all. For the marathon men, it also marks the southern terminus of Britain's first and toughest National Trail, the Pennine Way.

To the rock climber, its short but severe gritstone climbs are full of character and history, where some of the earliest climbers first tested their skills. Fell runners love the challenge offered by its shoe-sucking bogs and fierce ascents and descents.

To the naturalist, it is the first outpost of mountain Britain, an example of land 'at the end of its tether' but where rare and beautiful upland species like the mountain hare and cloudberry, reach their southern limit. To the botanist, it is a remarkable survival of a blanket bog – something which is now rarer, on an international scale, than the tropical rain forest.

To the conservationist, Kinder Scout holds a pivotal position in the history of the fight for National Parks and access to the countryside as the scene of the famous Mass Trespass in 1932, which is now seen as an important catalyst in the campaign for National Parks in Britain, but has also been the scene of some of the most innovative and successful moorland restoration work in Britain by the National Trust, its owner for the past 20 years.

*A*sk anyone in the outdoor world and they will usually have an opinion or an experience they want to share about Kinder. Love it or hate it, Kinder Scout is one of Britain's most important mountains. So at the start of the 21st century, what does its future hold?

The National Trust is determined that it should continue to be a place that people can enjoy and explore as an escape from the stresses and strains of everyday life; a place where people can seek refreshment and find adventure on their doorsteps, and a place where man-made barriers to access are as far as possible removed, whether those problems are physical or a lack of awareness or knowledge. But the Trust is also sure that it must be managed in a way which means people don't damage the very thing they've come to enjoy.

One of the biggest challenges facing the Trust in the future is how to make sure that everyone who wants to has the chance to get out and experience wild places like Kinder, because as Steve Trotter, the Trust's High Peak Estate Manager, points out, many are still excluded even today.

"Long ago, I lost count of the number of mature people who've come up to me and said: 'I still remember my first visit up Kinder when I was a youngster'– it is something which has always stayed with me."

"Indeed," admits Steve, *"I am one of them. The provision of appropriate information and advice to encourage lifelong learning based on first-hand experience is vitally important – and this is probably an area which we will concentrate on in the coming years."*

And he asks the question: *"Why shouldn't every child living within two hours of the Peak District be taken by their school to climb their nearest mountain and have a potentially life-changing experience?"*

Open access and the freedom to roam was secured for ever when the Trust bought the Kinder estate in October 1982. This was seen as a fitting tribute to the place which attracted the mass trespassers in 1932, and which inspired the birth of the wider access movement. The Trust foresees some minor footpath maintenance works being necessary in the future – on one or two of the popular edge and approach paths, but they say there will be no work undertaken on the central plateau.

*W*ork will also continue to support an even better range of wildlife, which should gradually develop and improve. The restoration of increasingly favourable moorland habitats for wildlife – through light grazing and rotational burning on heathery areas in winter – will continue at a low intensity.

A major reduction in the amounts of bare peat would be seen as a great achievement. *"Another sign that we are succeeding would be to see the merlin and twite take up summer residency in Broad Clough, or even better to see hen harriers breeding on Kinder,"* says Steve.

More broadleaved trees will be encouraged in some of the cloughs, but otherwise the plan is that Kinder will probably stay as most people would prefer it, as a more or less open moorland landscape. The water quality in Kinder's

GRINDSBROOK, SAFE FOR ALL TIME?

MORE BROADLEAVED TREES, SUCH AS THESE AUTUMNAL ROWANS IN THE VALLEY OF THE NOE, WILL BE ENCOURAGED

MRS. HUMPHREY WARD, THE HISTORY OF DAVID GRIEVE.

*No such colour as clothed that bronzed and reddish wall of rock, heather, and bilberry is known
to Westmoreland (sic), hardly to Scotland; it seems to be the peculiar property of the lonely and inaccessible district
which marks the mountainous centre mid-England – the district of Kinder Scout and the High Peak.*

streams and rivers will be used as an indicator of sound land management.

*K*inder is now protected by a whole battery of official designations: as an 'inalienable' National Trust property; part of the National Park; a Site of Special Scientific Interest; a Special Protection Area for birds, and it is soon to become a Special Area of Conservation for its unique peat bogs. But, of course, all these mean nothing if the moors are not managed properly – so fine tuning which is responsive to change is another key objective.

The Trust aims to prevent or minimize damaging impacts to the wildlife, recreational, landscape or historic interests of Kinder. Potentially the worst of these are uncontrolled fire or agricultural change, such as increased livestock numbers leading to overgrazing. But realistically, Steve admits that the Trust has little control over some of these.

Climate change, for example, could well pose a threat to Kinder as we know it. At present, the predictions are for wet, mild winters and long hot summers with frequent periods of drought. If this becomes a reality, moorland fires could become more frequent and severe, and new species could colonize the moors. Others, such as golden plover and ring ouzel, could well disappear. Red grouse, cloudberry, dunlin and others are at the south of their ranges on Kinder and may move north, while southern species such as the hobby could also move further north. If the climate gets wetter, this should favour the peat bogs, but similarly, if it gets drier, then we could expect more peat erosion.

Pollution can also have a major impact on the hills, but again this is very dependent on future technology and economic activity beyond Kinder. Perhaps if the trend for reduced levels of pollution continues, we will see sphagnum moss back on the Kinder plateau for the first time since the Industrial Revolution. As Steve points out: *"Who could have imagined that the soot fallout from chimneys that turned Kinder sheep a dirty black colour as recently as the 1950s would have been cleaned up so quickly?"*

Finally, now Kinder's historic landscape has been catalogued and recorded for the first time, it can be monitored and conserved from future damage or loss, except through the natural decay processes. The Kinder landscape is and always has been dynamic, and will continue to slowly evolve. All new National Trust initiatives,

"SOLITUDE AND ESTABLISHED STILLNESS, OLDER THAN THE WORLD." NOE STOOL, KINDER SCOUT

however, will be subject to the precautionary principle, to ensure that the precious aspects of Kinder continue to be protected.

So is Kinder Scout in safe hands now? Many outdoor types were worried when the National Trust acquired the estate two decades ago, fearing a sanitisation of Kinder's untamed wildnerness. They have been proved wrong; heather is now growing on Kinder where it had not been seen for 30 or 40 years, and the footpath restoration achieved by slabbing and pitching has generally weathered-in where the vegetation has grown back, and most is not as obtrusive as it once was.

Meanwhile, the gritstone tors, formed as compressed grit and gravel in northern rivers 300 million years ago, continue in their inexorable process to weather down to the sparkling quartzite sand in the paths, which will be washed down into the Noe, Derwent or Kinder rivers to start the immemorial process all over again.

And Kinder still offers for those who seek it that *"solitude and established stillness, older than the world"* as it always has, and it always will.

PREVIOUS PAGE: A NEW DAWN FOR KINDER? FROM GRINDSLOW KNOLL, LOOKING TOWARDS RINGING ROGER AND UPPER MOOR.

CREDITS AND
ACKNOWLEDGEMENTS

PHOTOGRAPHIC CREDITS

Kevin Borman: p10, 109
John Cleare, Moutain Camera: Back Cover
Karen Frenkel: p92
Gordon Gadsby: p10, 22, 23, 36, 40, 76, 101, 115, 118
John Gillham: p18, 20, 73
Mark Hamblin: p45, 46, 47, 49, 50, 57, 59
Paul Hobson: p52
Rod Leach: p6
Ray Manley, Peak District National Park: p2, 30, 31, 32, 34, 42, 43, 44, 48, 56, 57, 60, 66, 68, 69, 71, 75,
82, 84, 96, 97, 99, 116, 120, 136, 138, 142
Gordon Stainforth: p26, 110
National Trust, High Peak Estate: p16, 70, 122, 125, 127, 128, 129, 130, 134
Jerry Rawson: Front Cover, p12, 14, 15, 17, 19, 21, 24, 27, 33, 38, 54, 88, 91, 102, 105, 108, 112, 114, 124
Robin Weaver: p10, 28, 35, 41, 53, 58, 61, 62, 64, 74, 98, 118, 122, 126, 140

AUTHORS ACKNOWLEDGEMENTS

The biggest "thank you" should go to Stephen Lewis of New Mills, without whose original photographic exhibition this book would never have happened. Fiancial support was also received by New Mills Town Council and New Mills Heritage Centre.

The editor would also like to record his thanks to Robert Gent, Assistant Director of Derbyshire County Council Libraries and Heritage Service and Stephen Trotter, Manager of the National Trust's High Peak Estate, and Ken Vickers of Cordee Limited for their unfailing support for the project.

In addition, he would like to thank Sir Martin Doughty for so readily agreeing to write the foreword; to Jerry Rawson and Kevin Borman for their editorial assistance; to Jeremy Ashcroft for his perspective map used in the Routes to the Top feature, to Keith Warrenender for contributing historic pictures of the 1932 Mass Trespass, and to all the contributing authors and photographers for their unstinting enthusiasm for the project. I hope the result pleases them all.

Thanks are also due to Derbyshire County Council/David & Charles Limited, for permission to reproduce the excerpt from the reprinted First Edition Ordnance Survey map used on the front endpapers and to Harveys Maps, who produce a range of of maps especially for walkers and cyclists (Telephone 01786 841202 or www.harveymaps.co.uk), for the use of an excerpt from their Dark Peak North map on the back endpapers.